CITYSPOTS
HAMBURG

Paul Murphy

Written by Paul Murphy; introductory texts by Trevor Salisbury
Front cover photography courtesy of Getty Images

Produced by 183 Books
Design/layout/maps: Chris Lane and Lee Biggadike
Editorial/project management: Stephen York

Published by Thomas Cook Publishing
A division of Thomas Cook Tour Operations Limited
PO Box 227, Units 15/16, Coningsby Road
Peterborough PE3 8SB, United Kingdom
email: books@thomascook.com
www.thomascookpublishing.com
+44 (0)1733 416477

First edition © 2006 Thomas Cook Publishing
Text © 2006 Thomas Cook Publishing
Maps © 2006 Thomas Cook Publishing
ISBN-13: 978-1-84157-590-2
ISBN-10: 1-84157-590-9
Project Editor: Kelly Anne Pipes
Production/DTP: Steven Collins

Although every care has been taken in compiling this publication, and the contents are believed to be correct at the time of printing, Thomas Cook Tour Operations Limited cannot accept any responsibility for errors or omissions, however caused, or for changes in details given in this book, or for the consequences of any reliance on the information provided. Descriptions and assessments are based on the author's views and experiences at time of writing and do not necessarily represent those of Thomas Cook Tour Operations Limited.

Printed and bound in Spain by GraphyCems

CONTENTS

SYMBOLS & ABBREVIATIONS

The following symbols are used throughout this book:

☎ telephone	🖷 fax	🌐 website address
ⓐ address	🕒 opening times	Ⓝ public transport connections

The following symbols are used on the maps:

Ⓤ U-Bahn (subway)

Ⓢ S-Bahn (suburban trains)

🅸 Tourist Information Office

✈ Airport

Hotels and restaurants are graded by approximate price as follows:

€ budget **€€** mid-range **€€€** expensive

24-HOUR CLOCK

All times in this book are given in the 24-hour clock system used widely in Europe and in most international transport timetables.

◆ *Hamburg's busy docks seen from Landungsbrücken*

Introduction

The `Gateway to the World´ is the motto of the Free and Hanseatic City of Hamburg (to give it its full name) and its 104 areas certainly allow for some exploring. This old North Sea port is the second largest German city – only Berlin is larger – and like Berlin is not only a city but also one of the sixteen *Länder* or federal German states.

The city's history is an astonishing story of survival – Hamburg has overcome near-total destruction several times, the worst and most recent instance being the devastating firestorm and air raid of 1943. Yet there are few scars, and looking round the city centre and harbour there is little to hint at the troubled past – other than the stark stump of the St Nikolai church, left as a grim reminder.

Great ports usually have great nightlife, and Hamburg is no exception. The very name conjures up images of anything-goes St Pauli, the raunchy Reeperbahn, the Beatles at the Star Club. This side of the city is still thriving and, though perhaps a little more respectable these days, it won't disappoint you – Hamburgers still know how to enjoy themselves. Another bonus of Hamburg's maritime heritage is the cosmopolitan variety of its culture, not least in its restaurants – you can enjoy virtually the entire world's cuisines here. Finally, the connection with trade and the sea has bequeathed some superb sights and attractions, including fascinating museum ships and the unique Speicherstadt warehouse complex. Tourism is not the main industry of this hard-working, hard-playing, confident metropolis, but it is a hospitable and ouward-looking city that has been extending a welcome to overseas visitors for over eight centuries.

● *Nikolaifleet is one of Hamburg's many city-centre canals*

When to go

SEASONS & CLIMATE

Hamburg is worth visiting at any time of the year. Although the statistics tell us that the average temperature for the year only reaches 9.6°C (49°F), with 1.7°C (36°F) in January and 18.3°C (65°F) in July on average, these are only averages, and summer days can be much warmer (and winter days colder). The temperature in summer can certainly be high enough to tempt you to go bathing in one of the eight bathing lakes or 22 lidos. If you're visiting between early November and mid-March, pack your ice skates and join in the wintry fun at the skating rink in the Planten un Blomen Park.

Admittedly, it rains on average one day in every three in Hamburg but in summer, especially, you would be unlucky to be rained out more than a day, and in any case there's more than enough to do and see in Hamburg on a wet day (see page 48).

ANNUAL EVENTS

No matter what your interests are, you are certain to find an event to your taste. The following list represents only the most notable – there are plenty more of more specialist interest, which the Tourist Office and its website (see page 153) can provide information on.

March–April

Spring Market Month-long market on Heiligengeistfeld, St Pauli. 17 Mar–17 Apr 2006, 23 Mar–22 Apr 2007.

Olympus Marathon Starting and ending at the Hamburg Trade Fair grounds, coinciding with the Marathon & Running trade fair. 23 Apr 2006, 29 Apr 2007. Ⓦ www.marathon-hamburg.de For details of the fair Ⓦ www.hamburg-messe.de (navigate to Marathon & Running).

May–June
Port's Birthday Help Hamburg celebrate its birthday (see below).

HAMBURG'S BIRTHDAY

Hamburg celebrates the birthday of its port every May with a big gathering of ships, from yachts to stately clippers. A big birthday (Hamburg has been a port for over 800 years) demands a big party, and the event regularly attracts over a million visitors. In 1189 Emperor Friedrich Barbarossa issued the citizens of Hamburg with a charter, granting them an exemption from customs duties for their ships from the River Elbe to the North Sea, thereby opening Hamburg's gate to the world. The first celebrations, however, only took place in 1977. From a small start the event has continuously been expanded into the scale which can be witnessed today. Highlights are the church service, the grand entrance to the port by all of the participating ships and a fireworks display. Other items not to be missed are the tug ballet, in which tugboats actually dance along to music, and the dragon boat race.

On land it all happens along the Hafenmeile or 'Harbour mile' that stretches from the Speicherstadt to the fish market, providing space for food and entertainment for children and families. There's also a strong aerial element: visitors can also float in a hot air balloon, take a flight in a helicopter, watch parachuting or see how helicopters are used to save lives.

🕐 6–7 May 2006, 11–13 May 2007.

🌐 www.hafengeburtstag.de

Tennis Masters Series, held in Rotherbaum just north of the city centre. 8–14 May 2006, 7–13 May 2007.
Ⓦ www.dtb-tennis.de/AmRothenbaum
Hamburg Half-Marathon Run between Reeperbahn and Eppendorf. 25 Jun 2006 and 25 Jun 2007. Ⓦ www.hamburg-halbmarathon.de

July–August
Hummel Festival On the same site as the Spring Market. 28 Jul–27 Aug 2006, 27 Jul–26 Aug 2007. Ⓦ www.hamburger-dom.de
SchlagerMove Two-day 'Festival of Love' in St Pauli. Go back to the 60s and 70s and enjoy German pop music and a freaky party. The main event is on the second day, with a parade beginning at the

🔺 *You can buy all your presents and decorations at one of seven Christmas Markets in the city*

Hamburger Dom park. Ⓦ www.schlagermove.de (website is only in German but e-mail queries can be sent in English).

Vattenfall-Cyclassics Annual open cycling event in July. Ⓦ www.vattenfall-cyclassics.de (website is only in German but e-mail queries can be sent in English).

Alstervergnügen Binnenalster Amusement fair and fireworks festival from the last day of August into the first week of September. Ⓦ www.alstervergnuegen-hamburg.de

November–December

Tag der Kunstmeile (Art Mile Day) A mile of cultural centres and events to sample, almost for free, in mid-November. See page 20.

Christmas Markets From the middle of November up to Christmas Eve there is a historic Christmas market in front of the Rathaus (town hall) and six others at various sites around the city – for up-to-date details check Ⓦ www.hamburg-tourism.de

PUBLIC HOLIDAYS
New Year's Day 1 Jan
Good Friday 14 Apr 2006, 6 Apr 2007
Easter Monday 17 Apr 2006, 9 Apr 2007
Labour Day 1 May
Ascension Day 25 May 2006, 17 May 2007
Whit Monday 5 June 2006, 28 May 2007
Corpus Christi 15 June 2006, 7 June 2007
Day of Unity 3 Oct
All Saints' Day 1 Nov
Christmas 25 & 26 Dec

The Beatles in Hamburg

In 1960 John Lennon, Paul McCartney, George Harrison, Stu Sutcliff (on bass) and Pete Best (on drums) were a fairly rough-and-ready band without a proper name who weren't getting many gigs in Liverpool. They were asked to go to Hamburg, where other Liverpool bands were popular, and jumped at the chance. 'The Reeperbahn and the Grosse Freiheit were the best things we'd ever seen' said George later. 'There were seedy things about it, obviously, including some of the conditions we had to live in when we first got there.'

The band first played at the Indra at 64 Grosse Freiheit (still there) and it was here that they adopted the name The Beatles. They lived just around the corner off the top of Grosse Freiheit at 33 Paul-Roosen Strasse in the Bambi Kino (cinema) – 'a pigsty' in John's words – also still in existence. They moved from the Indra to the Kaiserkeller (see page 122), where they met Ringo, and stayed here until their work permit expired. The following year they returned to

Hamburg and played the Top Ten Club, at 136 Reeperbahn (still here, next to the Reeperbahn S-Bahn) and the Star Club, which was to be their most famous venue. In 1962 they returned to the Star Club three times, in January, November and December. Their last gig in Hamburg was 31 December 1962. The original Star Club burned down many years ago and only a plaque now marks the site where the Beatles, Jimmy (sic) Hendrix, Ray Charles, Gene Vincent, Bo Diddley and many other music legends played. You'll find it opposite the Kaiserkeller through an archway in a small courtyard.

For more on this seminal and fascinating period in the life of the Fab Four, buy the audio CD The Savage Young Beatles in Hamburg 1961: A Musical Biography, which is a first–hand account including reminiscences from most of the people who were there. There is also a guided walking tour The Beatles in St Pauli – a Magical Mystery Tour (see box, page 112).

● *Grosse Freiheit's clubland is where the Beatles were born*

History

When looking at today's Hamburg it is difficult to believe that this was just a village in the 9th century and that it had to withstand numerous bouts of destruction before it became what it is today. Evidence of a Saxon settlement dating back to the 4th century AD has been found above the Elbe estuary but the first castle, the Hammaburg, was erected in the 9th century close to the Alster estuary in a village named Hamm (now Domplatz).

It had already survived two large fires (one on 5 August 1284 which broke out in the old part of the town and one almost 600 years later on 5–8 May 1842, resulting in a loss of one-third of the city) before the devastating air-raid and firestorm of 1943 all but razed it to the ground (see page 68), and a great flood as recently as 16–17 February 1962 resulted in 315 deaths and 150,000 citizens being cut off.

But all was not bad in the city on the Elbe. After all, it has been a flourishing port for centuries, was a key member of the great Hanseatic League of German trading cities and had its own merchant fleet. It obviously had to contend with pirates, the most famous being Klaus Störtebeker, who has become something of a legend in North German history, seen by many as a kind of maritime Robin Hood who stole from the rich to give it to the poor. His career was put to an end when he was surprised by ships heading for England and was taken prisoner and beheaded on 21 October 1400 at Grasbrook in Hamburg, where a monument marks the spot. Evidence of the flourishing trade relations which Hamburg had with other areas of the globe is shown by the fact that it also attracted English merchants, who opened up branches here in the second half of the 16th century.

The success continued for the next four centuries, with a few interruptions, such as Napoleon's attempts to suppress its trade with Britain. The first steamship came from England in 1816 and the first railway line was constructed in 1842; in 1847, The Hamburg-Amerikanischen Packetfahrt-Actien-Gesellschaft, better known by its initials HAPAG, was founded. World War I severely dented the success story: Hamburg was forced to give up its merchant fleet, and that after having lost 40,000 men in the war. Hamburg revived in the inter-war years but in World War II Allied air-raids destroyed almost 50 per cent of the housing and 80 per cent of the port and killed an estimated 45,000 people. When the 7th British Tank Division entered Hamburg, they found 1.1 million survivors living among massive destruction. Post-war reconstruction and Hamburg's commercial resilience makes this hard to believe when you look at the city today.

⬤ *Hamburg's story is told at the excellent Hamburg History Museum*

Lifestyle

Hamburg is a cosmopolitan seaport and industrial centre of more than 1.7 million inhabitants. Like large ports everywhere, it has seen visitors of every culture and nationality for centuries and this has resulted in an outward-looking, tolerant and worldly-wise attitude among its citizens. The fact that it has a student population of over 60,000 helps keep the atmosphere lively, and 15 per cent of Hamburg's population are immigrants, giving the city a cosmopolitan outlook.

Generally speaking, people in Hamburg are very friendly, making it easy to start a conversation with them, especially since English is the main foreign language in German schools, so that the majority of younger people also speak English to a lesser or greater extent. Nevertheless, social etiquette is a little more formal than British and North American visitors may be used to. It is normal, even among younger people, to shake hands when you meet and again when departing as a gesture of friendship. This is even customary among relatives when they visit each other.

Hamburg is famous for its nightlife – *In Hamburg sind die Nächte lang*, 'In Hamburg the nights are long', goes the German saying – and the notoriety of parts of the St Pauli, especially the Reeperbahn, are another legacy of the city's historic role as a home from home for the world's sailors. In fact Hamburg offers every kind of entertainment, from high-brow classical music and theatre to cutting-edge pop, and a whole-hearted appetite for life, whether it be food and drink, the company of friends or sports and activities of every kind, characterises the people of this energetic city, and belying the stereotype, common even in its home country, of the dour North German character. Like most Germans, Hamburgers are great joiners, belonging to large numbers of clubs and societies – not only the traditional sports clubs but associations for all interests, from allotment gardening to American square dancing.

Hamburg is not only Germany's second-biggest city but also its undisputed media centre, home to most of Germany's largest newspaper and book publishing empires and over 6000 companies in the realm of film, radio and TV.

⬤ *A night in the pub is all the nightlife many Hamburgers want*

Culture

Hamburg has a lot to offer by way of culture. Theatres, museums, musical theatres and concerts: everything is there.

Visitors who would like to know more about the history of Hamburg and past life there could visit one of the almost 90 museums and collections. Here you are certain to find something which interests you. These include a Wine Museum, a museum dedicated to Johannes Brahms, a Museum for Hamburg History, one for Ethnology, two museum ships and even a museum submarine.

Even Ohlsdorf Cemetery has a museum, and if none of this interests you, you can always try the Erotic Art Museum.

You have just as wide a choice if you are a theatre-goer. Hamburg is home to no less than 34 theatres, offering everything from cabaret to puppet shows. It doesn't matter if you don't speak German – the English Theatre stages plays in English, from Shakespeare to Pinter and even Noel Coward – between September and June. If you are around in September you can sample the whole

The Kunsthalle's galleries range from medieval art to 21st-century installations

gamut of Hamburg drama in the Long Theatre Night, when you have the opportunity of going in and out of various performances.

Hamburg is also big on musicals – *Dance of the Vampires*, *Mamma Mia* and *The Lion King* are just some of the long-running favourites. Concerts abound throughout the year at venues ranging from churches to the Colorline Arena (see page 34) and the Congress Centre.

A highlight of the Hamburg cultural calendar has to be the Tag der Kunstmeile (Art Mile Day). On a date in November (check website for details), the Kunsthalle (Arts Hall), the Museum für Kunst und Gewerbe (Arts and Trade Museum), the Galerienhaus (Gallery House), the Kunsthaus (House of Art), the Kunstverein (Art Association), the Freie Akademie der Künste (Free Academy of the Arts) the Deichtor halls, Gallerie 1 of the Hamburg Savings Bank (Haspa) and the central library, which are all situated along the 1.5 km (1 mile) route between the Alster and the Harbour, invite visitors to come in and take a look around between 10.00 and 24.00. Performances, concerts, short guided tours of the premises and a party are all on offer. The visitors also do not have to worry about getting back either, as shuttle buses are provided every half hour between 11 am and midnight.

Tag der Kunstmeile ⓦ www.hamburg.de/behoerden/museen/kmh

Above all, culture is seen as fun in Hamburg – and hardly an event is staged which doesn't involve a closing party. The range of cultural attractions is so wide that you need to narrow it down a little and check out what's happening when you are due to visit: make the Tourist Office or its website your first stop (see page 153).

---

❶ *Relaxing near the Jungfernstieg*

Shopping

For as long as your enthusiasm, energy or credit card lasts, Hamburg can be one long shopping spree. As befits one of the world's greatest historical trading centres, the city is a consumer paradise.

WHERE TO BUY

The main shopping street is Mönckebergstrasse, near the central railway station, with a wide range of stores. Hamburg is home to many fashion outlets, such as Benetton in Rosenstrasse and Bergstrasse or Esprit, which has a store in the Elbe shopping centre and five others in various parts of Hamburg. Another possibility is a second-hand store such as Suspekt in the Carolinen Quarter (❸ Marktstrasse), which sells fashion from the 50s, 60s and 70s together with a number of accessories.

If the weather should be bad or you simply like the flair of shopping centres, then you have the choice of ten, one of the largest being the Elbe shopping centre in the Osdorfer Landstrasse. Here you can choose from more than 120 shops on two floors.

MARKETS

Despite its name, you can buy almost anything at the Sunday Fish Market in St Pauli – and fish, of course.

A flea market selling antiques and other collectables in an area of 500 sq m (5382 sq ft) is situated close to the Museum der Arbeit (Work Museum) and is held seven times a year. More frequent is the market held at Von-Melle-Park at the university from 08.00 to 16.00 every Saturday.

Fish Market ◷ Sun 05.00–09.30 mid-Mar–mid-Nov; 07.00–09.30 mid-Nov–mid-Mar.

USEFUL SHOPPING PHRASES

What time do the shops open/close?
Um wieviel Uhr öffnen/schliessen die Geschäfte?
Oom veefeel oor erffnen/shleessen dee geshefter?

How much is this?
Wieviel kostet das?
Veefeel kostet das?

Can I try this on?
Kann ich das anprobieren?
Can ikh das anprobeeren?

My size is ...
Ich habe Grösse ...
Ikh haber grerser ...

I'll take this one, thank you
Ich nehme das, danke schön
Ikh neymer das, danker shern

Can you show me the one in the window/this one?
Zeigen Sie mir bitte das im Fenster/dieses da?
Tsyegen zee mere bitter dass im fenster/deezess dar?

WHAT TO BUY

Something maritime makes an appropriate souvenir of this city. A old favourite is the ship in a bottle; at **Binikowski** (Ⓔ Lokstedter Weg) you can choose from around 200 different models.

Shopping for German food, wine and beer is a delight, whether at a specialist *Delikatessen* or in the food halls of the big stores. Many local specialities, such as *Würstchen* (sausages) and other cooked meats, are packaged in a way that makes them easy to take home as edible souvenirs. There is even a shop called Sandy´s in the Stresemannstrasse in Altona which sells English food.

Eating & drinking

Hamburg claims to be the gastronomic capital of Germany, and the national gourmet magazine *Feinschmecker* recently confirmed that. It's not surprising, perhaps, that a metropolis which has been Germany's gateway to the world for centuries should be able to offer a vast range of national cuisines, or that the country's media capital should boast some of its very best restaurants.

WHERE TO EAT

An establishment calling itself a *Restaurant* is likely to be fairly upmarket (but not necessarily, especially if it's an ethnic restaurant); more traditional places are more likely to be called a *Gasthof* or *Gaststätte*.

Options for simpler food, which may also include a breakfast menu, are a *Brauhaus* (traditionally a place where the range and quality of the beers is paramount), a *Kneipe* (a pub – choice of food may be limited), a café or a bistro. Wherever you go, the standards of hygiene and service are likely to be high, and the portions generous. Bear in mind that the more modest establishments may not take credit cards.

If all you want is coffee and cake, you can drop in not only at a café but also at almost any bakery (*Bäckerei*), where you can choose

RESTAURANT PRICE CATEGORIES

Ratings used in the book are based on the average cost per person of a 3-course meal, without drinks.

€ under €25 €€ €25–€35 €€€ = over €35

from a delicious range of calorie-laden cakes (*Kuchen*) or filled tarts (*Torte*) and eat it at a table as you sip your coffee.

LOCAL SPECIALITIES

Look for *Hamburgisch* on the menu to find an authentic taste of Hamburg. Naturally enough, Hamburg makes much of its fish dishes, and many traditional-style restaurants will have a wider range of these than, say, in inland Germany. Eel (*Aal*) dishes are popular, while one of the city's most intriguing dishes is *Labskaus*, a kind of seaman's stew, which may contain beef and/or herring stewed with a variety of vegetables. It appears to be the same dish known in Liverpool as lobscouse (hence 'scouser' as a nickname for Liverpudlians), though which great seaport exported it to the other is unclear.

● *Much of the excellent seafood on sale at the Fischmarkt ends up on restaurant tables*

FAST FOOD & BUDGET EATING

If you're hungry for the products of Pizza Hut and McDonalds, you'll find them in Hamburg, and they'll taste exactly like the ones back home. Local alternatives for cheap eats are the thirteen *Nordsee* fish restaurants scattered around the city, where you can either eat in or take away at prices starting at around €4, and the Schweinske restaurants in many parts of Hamburg, one being situated inside the railway station. Here, you will be served by young friendly staff with a wide choice of meals, including breakfast. They offer an excellent range of veal dishes, all under €10 and Germany's most popular fast food, *Currywurst* – simply a frankfurter-style sausage in a curry sauce. To tell the truth, the food in most pubs and local restaurants is far from expensive, and usually plentiful; visitors on a budget are unlikely to leave Hamburg hungry or starved of choice.

INTERNATIONAL & VEGETARIAN CUISINE

With its cosmopolitan population, it's not hard to find ethnic

HOME OF THE HAMBURGER?

Despite the name, Hamburg's local cuisine has no particular affinity with what we call hamburgers (which are known as *Frikadelle* in Germany). Similar dishes have been cooked all over the world since time immemorial, though there is some evidence that the cheap ground beef dish originally called a 'Hamburg steak' was first popularised among the transient seagoing population of the port of Hamburg, and as a 'Hamburger' made its first appearance in the USA for sale to German sailors on the New York waterfront.

cuisines of all kinds in Hamburg. Vegetarians traditionally have had a hard time finding places to eat in meat-loving Germany, but there's usually no trouble locating vegetarian options in Chinese, Thai or Indian restaurants. Even more locally inspired restaurants are coming round to the idea of vegetarian options, and it's always worth asking, as most places will turn out a decent salad. The following establishments are not exclusively vegetarian but make a point of advertising veggie options:

Anno 1905 Schank- und Speisewirtschaft € Splendidly named restaurant in Altona with lovely traditional décor, with a speciality in local cuisine as well as vegetarian dishes. ⓐ Holstenplatz 17. ⓣ 439 2535.

Restaurant Erich € *Gasthof* in St Pauli with a range of international dishes. Takes credit cards. ⓐ Bernhard-Nocht-Strasse 69. ⓣ 317 8060.

Shalimar € Cosy Indian restaurant in Rotherbaum, just north of the city centre. Credit cards accepted. ⓐ Dillstrasse 16. ⓣ 442484.

PICNICS

One of the benefits of the amount of green space within the city is the opportunity it gives for a do-it-yourself lunch – or even a barbecue. Favourite places include the Aussenalster in the city centre, the Planten un Blomen Park and even the yacht harbour in Wedel. The most inexpensive places to buy food for a picnic are discount grocery stores such as Lidl, Aldi or Plus. Better-quality fare, including ready-to-eat dishes, can be obtained at specialist delicatessens and the food departments of large department stores, which are always of a very high standard.

DRINKS

Since the closure of Hamburg's Bavaria plant, which brewed the enticingly named 'St Pauli Girl', the Hamburg brewing scene is dominated by the internationally distributed Holsten brewery, a subsidiary of Carlsberg, but many other German brands are on sale, too. However, if you are looking for something more special, check out the Brauhäuser, some of which are true microbreweries. One to try is the Gröninger Braukeller & Brauhaus Hanseat Dehns Privatbrauerei (see page 101).

International soft-drink brands are available everywhere; if you want a Coke, ask for 'Cola'. If a beer is too heavy on a warm midday, order an 'Alster Wasser', beer and lemonade – shandy, in other words.

ETIQUETTE & TIPPING

Except in the more upscale restaurants, you can normally choose your own table and sit down, rather than wait to be shown to it (unless of course the place is so busy you have to stand until the waiter points out a free table). A traditional *Gasthof* or pub may have a table marked *Stammtisch*. Even if it's empty and the rest of the place is busy, don't sit there: it's for regular patrons only. Normally expect to give 5–10 per cent of the total bill in restaurants; not necessary if service is shown as included, but a rounding-up to the next euro (if under 50 cents) is appreciated. In pubs and bars, especially more traditional ones, your waiter may mark your beermat each time you order drinks and then count up the bill from it at the end of the session; a small tip at the end of your evening's drinking is a good idea, especially if you plan on returning.

USEFUL DINING PHRASES

I would like a table for ... people
Ein Tisch für ... Personen, bitte
Ine teesh foor ... perzohnen, bitter

Waiter/waitress!
Herr Ober/Fräulein, bitte!
Hair ohber/froyline, bitter!

May I have the bill, please?
Die Rechnung, bitte?
Dee rekhnung, bitter?

Could I have it well-cooked/medium/rare please?
Ich möchte es bitte durch/halb durch/englisch gebraten?
Ikh merkhter es bitter doorkh/halb doorkh/eng-lish gebrarten?

I am a vegetarian. Does this contain meat?
Ich bin Vegetarier (Vegetarierin fem.). Enthält das hier Fleisch?
Ish bin veggetaareer (veggetaareerin). Enthelt dass heer flyshe?

Where is the toilet (restroom) please?
Wo sind die Toiletten, bitte?
Voo zeent dee toletten, bitter?

I would like a cup of/two cups of/another coffee/tea, please
Eine Tasse/Zwei Tassen/noch eine Tasse Kaffee/Tee, bitte
Ikh merkhter iner tasser/tsvy tassen kafey/tey, bitter

I would like a beer/two beers, please
Ein Bier/Zwei Biere, bitte
Ine beer/tsvy beerer, bitter

Entertainment & nightlife

Hamburg is a night-time kind of place and there's no excuse for being bored, whether you are into ballet or hip-hop, a quiet drink or a dancing the night away. The statistics speak for themselves: at the last count Hamburg could offer 91 bars, 21 clubs, 44 discos, not to mention cinemas, theatres and all the restaurants, local pubs and cafés. Most nightlife is concentrated in the city centre and the St Pauli district.

Cinema

You can watch the latest releases in English at Grindel UFA, in the University Quarter. Tickets can be reserved by phone.

Grindel-UFA ⓐ Grindelberg 7a. ⓣ 449 333. ⓦ www.ufa-grindel.de
ⓝ U-bahn: Hohe Luftbrücke.

⬥ *Even the Fish Market is an entertainment venue*

Theatre

Hamburg has a lively English-language theatre scene. including the long-established English Theatre.

English Theatre ⓐ Lerchenfeld 14. ⓣ 227 7089.
ⓦ www.englishtheatre.de ⓝ U-Bahn: Mundsburg.

Opera & ballet

Visitors who prefer to go to an opera or watch a ballet performance are also catered for at the Hamburg State Opera and the Hamburg Ballet, both of them international-class venues. Bookings can be made on-line or by phone, or from one of the 25 ticket shop agencies around Hamburg, including some in travel agencies.

Hamburg State Opera & Ballet ⓐ Grosse Theaterstrasse 25.
ⓣ 35 68 68 (box office). ⓦ www.hamburgische-staatsoper.de
www.hamburgballett.de/e/

Bars, clubs & discos

Hamburg has a total of 91 bars and 21 clubs on offer to fun-seekers, so that there is certain to be something to meet all tastes. Hamburg is also home to a large number of discos, 44 of them in the St Pauli district alone. There is a wide choice of all kinds of music including R&B, techno and reggae.

Th epicentre of the Hamburg bar and club scene is Grosse Freiheit, in the heart of St Pauli, but other streets to browse include the Spielbudenplatz and, of course, the Reeperbahn. Outside St Pauli the pace of nightlife is perhaps not quite so hot, but there are still plenty of options in the city centre and the Schanzen district, lying strategically between St Pauli and the University area.

WHAT'S ON

Pick up a free copy of *Hamburg: Pur* from the tourist office for all nightlife listings or buy *Szene* from a newsagent. Both publications are in German only but it's easy to work out what's happening where. *Szene* also reviews places to eat and drink (Ⓦ www.szene-hamburg-online.de).

English-language cinema and theatre links can be found at
Ⓦ www.englishpages.de

Ⓦ www.bartime.de provides information on all of the bars and even awards ratings for them.

◑ *No trip to Hamburg would be complete without a night-time stroll down Grosse Freiheit*

heit Nr. 7

GER E

GO GO

DA

DOLLHOU

TAB

Safari

SSE FRE

36

Sport & relaxation

SPECTATOR SPORTS

Football is probably Hamburg's number one spectator sport, and Hamburg SV has for long been one in the Bundesliga's top flight. Home games are played, usually on Saturday afternoons at the 55,000-seater AOL Arena, near Stellingen in the north-western suburbs, upgraded since Hamburg was chosen as one of the cities to stage the 2006 World Cup Finals.

Hamburg SV Tickets can be obtained on-line at ⓦ www.hsv.com and on ❶ 41 55 01.

American football is also popular: Hamburg Blue Devils play at the eVendi Arena, not far from the AOL Arena for more info visit ⓦ www.h-b-d.com). Ice hockey also has a big following in the city. The Hamburg Freezers play at the Color Line Arena, also near the new World Cup Stadium.

FITNESS & WELLNESS

In Hamburg you can keep fit and see the city at the same time. TouristJogging offers jogging tours to city visitors, as individuals or groups (three or more people are offered a 50 per cent discount). This might also be a good way of training for the Hamburg Olympus Marathon (see page 8)

TouristJogging ❸ Schanzenstrasse 41a, Haus 9. ❶ 439 87 80. ⓦ www.touristjogging.de

If jogging is too strenuous for you, then why not try the Hamburg Nordic Walking Park in Alstertal. This was opened in September 2004 and offers ten different routes of varying levels of difficulty. The walks start at three points: the Marriot Hotel Treudelberg, Wellingsbüttel Gatehouse and close to the adventure playground in the Wellingsbüttler LandStrasse.

A good way of relaxing is to visit one of the 11 spas situated around the city, inluding the ultimate in pampering at the Hotel Kempinski Grand Atlantic (see page 39). Hamburg Tourism (see page 153) also offer wellness packages at the city's hotels.

The AOL Arena – a stadium fit for the World Cup Finals

Accommodation

Being a major trade and congress centre, the city's accommodation is skewed to the more expensive end of the market, but Hamburg still offers something for all pockets.

PRICE RATINGS

Hotels in Germany are graded according to a voluntary 1–5 star rating system, which conforms to international standards. The ratings in this book are based on the average price for a double room, per night, as follows:

€ under €50 €€ €51–€100 €€€ over €100

HOTELS

Frauenhotel Hanseatin € Close to the Congress Centre. The only Hamburg hotel which accepts solely female guests (apart from children up to the age of 7).
ⓐ Dragonerstall 11. ① 34 13 45. ⓦ www.frauenhotels.de/hanse.htm

Hotel Stern € Situated directly on Reeperbahn, close to the port and the fish market, perfect for night owls and club-hoppers.
ⓐ Reeperbahn 154. ① 31 76 99 90. ⓦ www.stern-hamburg.de

25 Hours Hotel €€ Designed in the style of the 60s and 70s and self-consciously cool. Stages lots of rock and pop events and parties. Situated in Altona. ⓐ Paul-Dessau-Strasse 2. ① 85 50 70.
ⓦ www.25hours-hotel.com

Auto-Parkhotel Hamburg €€ In a quiet location but still close to Reeperbahn and a short walk from the Fish Market. On-site parking. ❷ Lincolnstrasse 8. ❶ 31 00 24. ❿ www.auto-parkhotel-hamburg.de

Best Western Hotel Hamburg International €€ Free parking, own restaurant and bar. Fast underground connection to the city centre. ❷ Hammer Landstrasse 200–202. ❶ 21 04 30; ❿ www.hotel-hamburg.bestwestern.de

Fritzhotel €€ 17 rooms all with different designs. The hip Schanzen District starts on the doorstep. ❷ Schanzenstrasse 101–103. ❶ 82 22 28 30. ❿ www.fritzhotel.com

Hotel Fürst Bismarck €€ Situated opposite the main railway station, close to the Schauspielhaus and Kunsthalle. ❷ Kirchenallee 49. ❶ 28 01 09 1. ❿ www.fuerstbismarck.de

Hotel Graf Moltke Hamburg €€ Centrally located in St Georg, close to the Alster, museums, the theatre and shopping passages. ❷ Steindamm 1. ❶ 28 01 15 4. ❿ www.hotel-graf-moltke.de

Hotel Helgoland Hamburg €€ Three-star hotel with 110 rooms. Situated close to Hagenbeck Zoological Gardens. ❷ Kieler Strasse 173–177. ❶ 85 70 01. ❿ www.hotel-helgoland.de

Hotel Kronprinz €€ 70 rooms furnished in a traditional style. Situated opposite the main railway station. ❷ Kirchenallee 46. ❶ 27 14 07 0. ❿ www.kronprinz-hamburg.de

Hotel Norddeutscher Hof €€ Centrally situated, only a few hundred

metres from the railway station. ⓐ Kirchenallee 24. ⓣ 24 56 10.
ⓦ www.hotel-norddeutscher-hof.de

Hotel St Annen €€ A few minutes from the Port, Fish Market and
Reeperbahn on foot, and from the city centre by U-Bahn. Has a garden
terrace. ⓐ Annenstrasse 5. ⓣ 31 77 13 0. ⓦ www.hotel-st-annen.de

Ibis Hotel Hamburg Altona €€ Familiar formula of this popular
chain, good value without being in the least exciting or different.
Has an on-site café. There are other Ibis hotels in St Pauli, at the
airport and other suburbs. ⓐ Koenigstrasse 4. ⓣ 31 187 0.
ⓦ www.ibishotel.com

Ökotel Hamburg €€ What's an eco-hotel? One where all the room
furnishings are of natural material, all the food served is from
biologically cultivated ingredients and served with bio-wine and
eco-beer. The promise is 'an ecological lifestyle without renunciation
of comfort'. Situated in Schnelsen. ⓐ Holsteiner Chaussee 347.
ⓣ 55 97 30 0. ⓦ www.oekotel.de

Hotel Wedina €€–€€€ Close to the main railway station. The
novelty here is that the hotel has a strong literary bias; the list of
well known authors who have stayed here is endless, and the hotel
even offers author readings. Breakfast can be taken in the garden.
ⓐ Gurlittstrasse 23. ⓣ 28 08 90 0. ⓦ www.wedina.de

Nippon Hotel €€–€€€ This is a hotel for fans of the Japanese way
of life. All of the rooms are designed with Japan in mind. The
location is in Uhlenhorst, a few minutes from the city centre.
ⓐ Hofweg 75. ⓣ 22 71 14 0. ⓦ www.nippon-hotel-hh.de

East €€€ New, ultra-stylish, orientally themed hotel in St Pauli, one block north of the Reeperbahn. State-of-the-art wellness centre, fine oriental cuisine. ⓐ Simon-von-Utrecht-Strasse 31. ⓣ 30 99 30. ⓦ www.east-hamburg.de

Garden Hotel €€€ From here, there is a jetty enabling the visitor to visit the Thalia theatre, State Opera or Jungfernstieg by boat. It is even possible to control the electronic blinds without getting out of bed. Situated in Pöseldorf. ⓐ Magdalenenstrasse 60. ⓣ 41 40 40. ⓦ www.gardenhotels.de

Hotel Elysee €€€ A short walk from the centre, this privately owned five-star luxury hotel caters mostly for business people but is cheerful, bright and lively and the staff are friendly and efficient. Rooms are attractive and very comfortable and facilities include a brand new Wellness Centre. ⓐ Rothenbaumchaussee 10. ⓣ 41 41 20. ⓦ www.elysee.de

Hotel Hafen Hamburg €€€ In a perfect position for harbour-watching, this landmark hotel towers above the Landungsbrücken. It is a mix of old and new, with several different styles and sizes of room, so choose carefully but do try to get a room at the front! Non-residents can enjoy great views from its Restaurant Port and its Tower Bar (see page 101). ⓐ Seewartenstrasse. ⓣ 31 11 30. ⓦ www.hotel-hamburg.de

Hotel Kempinski Grand Atlantic €€€ This Grand Hotel, opened in 1909, is a Hamburg landmark and enjoys the perfect city centre setting, right on the Innenalster lake. It was made famous by James Bond (Pierce Brosnan) who clambered over its famous roof in

Tomorrow Never Dies. The old-world glamour of its high-ceilinged stuccoed rooms is complemented by modern efficiency and superb restaurants (see Tsao Tang, page 87). ➋ An der Alster 72–79. ➊ 28 880. Ⓦ www.atlantic.de

Hotel Louis C Jacobs €€€ One of The Leading Small Hotels of the World association. Guests come here to experience the discreet lifestyle of a Hanseatic shipping magnate in some of Germany's most luxurious suites and rooms. It is set a little way out of town on the beautiful Elbchausee near Blankenese and enjoys wonderful views from its linden-shaded terrace. The food is exceptional (see page 123), the service is perfect. ➋ Elbchausee 401–403. ➊ 822 550. Ⓦ www.hotel-jacobi.de

Hotel Side €€€ Cool and trendy with arty 60s-influenced minimalist public areas, beautiful designer bedrooms and superb wellness facilities, this city centre hotel is a paragon of early 21st-century style and efficiency. First-class service from a young, confident staff. Their Fusion bar restaurant offers excellent east-meets-west cuisine.
➋ Drehbahn 49. ➊ 30 99 90. Ⓦ www.side-hamburg.de

Junges Hotel €€€ 135-room hotel situated close to the main railway station. Has a sauna, solarium and roof terrace. ➋ Kurt-Schumacher-Allee 14. ➊ 41 92 30. Ⓦ www.junges-hotel.de

Raffles Vier Jahreszeiten €€€ Hamburg's belle époque queen of hotels has taken on a new lease of life since being acquired by the Singapore-based Raffles group. Very central, very luxurious.
➋ Neuer Jungfernstieg 9–14 ➊ 34 94 0. Ⓦ www.raffles-hvj.de

YoHo €€€ Despite its tagline 'the young hotel' and its marketing slant towards younger visitors, this is no cheap hostel. It offers 30 fairly luxurious rooms in a modernised villa in the fashionable Schanzen District. Pricing is according to age, and under-27s get a better deal. ⓐ Moorkamp 5. ⓣ 28 41 91 0. ⓦ www.yoho-hamburg.de

YOUTH HOSTELS
Auf dem Stintfang Youth Hostel € This hostel offers 2-4-bed rooms and has a view of the port of Hamburg. ⓐ Alfred-Wegener-Weg 5. ⓣ 31 34 88. ⓦ http://lbs.hh.schule.de/djh/jhstintfang.htm

Horner Rennbahn € Offers 2–6-bed rooms, is next to a racecourse and just five U-Bahn stops from the city centre. ⓐ Rennbahnstrasse 100. ⓣ 65 11 67 1. ⓦ http://lbs.hh.schule.de/djh/jghhamburg.htm

Instant Sleep Hostel € 12 rooms, 45 beds, especially for backpackers. Situated in the happening Schanzen district. Has local transport connections via the S5 S-Bahn. Kitchen provided, as are washing machines. No closing times. ⓐ Max-Brauer-Allee 277. ⓣ 43 18 23 10. ⓦ www.instantsleep.de

CAMPSITES
Buchholz € 40 spaces, in a residential area with fast connections to the city. Open all year. ⓐ Kieler Strasse 374. ⓣ 54 04 532. ⓦ www.camping-buchholz.de

Schnelsen-Nord € A well equipped site offering 145 spaces, close to a large Swedish furniture store and not too far from the airport. ⓐ Wunderbrunnen 2. ⓣ 55 94 22 5 7; ⓦ www.campingplatz-hamburg.de

THE BEST OF HAMBURG

If you only have a few days to spend in Hamburg, take a bus tour to give you an overview of the city. Several tours depart from Landungsbrücken or at the rear of the main railway station, Hauptbahnhof. Also enquire at the Tourist Office about guided walks in English.

TOP 10 ATTRACTIONS
Ten experiences you shouldn't miss on any trip to Hamburg.

- **Friday or Saturday night in St Pauli** It's tacky, fun for many and offensive to some, though in recent years it has cleaned up its act. You haven't seen Hamburg until you've been here (see page 117).

- **Harbour Tour** Hamburg owes its prosperity, past and present, to its maritime trade, so a trip around the harbour is essential. The scale alone is impressive (see page 90).

- **Cruise on the Alster lake** Choose a sunny day and take the Alster-Kreuz-Fahrten, a leisurely 2-hour cruise. Hop off to visit fashionable lakeside cafés and restaurants or take a picnic and eat in the Alsterpark (see pages 62 and 64).

- **The Hamburg History Museum** You can save this for a rainy day but really it should be one of your first stops. It's lively,

very informative, very impressive and all exhibits have English captions (see page 69).

- **Jazz session** Hamburg is known for its love of jazz and there's something very *gemütlich* about a crowded little jazz bar with an appreciative crowd.

- **Sunday Fish Market** Even non-German speakers will smile at the banter at this lively weekly event. Good street food, live music, souvenirs and great food bargains (see page 114).

- **Speicherstadt** The world's biggest warehouse complex is still only in its infancy as a tourist attraction but already there is enough here to warrant putting it on your A list (see page 95).

- **Michaeliskirche** at 12 noon for the three-organ concert, ascending the tower for the views over the port then stepping next door to see the 17th-century almshouses (see page 70).

- **Blankenese**, for its hilly 'Staircase Quarter', messing about on the beach and finishing the day in a thatched tearoom (see page 126).

- **Lübeck** Make time for a day out to this beautiful, well-preserved historic city (see page 130).

🔽 *A classic view of Hamburg Rathaus through the arches of Alsterarkaden*

Here's a quick guide to seeing the best of Hamburg, depending on the time available.

HALF-DAY: HAMBURG IN A HURRY

Go to the lakeside at Jungfernstieg and take a 1-hour tour of the picturesque Alster lake. The views back to the city centre are excellent, you will get a commentary not only about the Alster and its grand houses but about the city too. Back on shore take the U-Bahn or S-Bahn (it doesn't matter which) from Jungfernstieg station to Landungsbrücken, where you have a panoramic view of the docks. Take a walk along the front on the floating landing stages, grabbing a fish sandwich en route. From here you can go back to Jungfernstieg for shopping, or continue the maritime theme by visiting the *Rickmer-Rickmers* or *Cap San Diego* museum ships.

1 DAY: TIME TO SEE A LITTLE MORE

If you would rather see big ships than big houses, take a harbour tour instead of the lake tour and see the Alster by a one-hour bus tour instead. Both depart from the Landungsbrücken, so you can step from one straight to the other. While you are at the docks, however, you may wish to make the short detour (5–10-minute walk) to Deichstrasse to see Hamburg's oldest surviving buildings, where you can also get lunch, then cross the river to the Speicherstadt warehouse complex, where the Spice Museum is recommended.

2–3 DAYS: SHORT CITY BREAK

With more time in hand you can start to get under the skin of this fascinating city and you will also have a better chance of dry weather/wet weather options. Use the dry weather options for tours on the water, though it is probably best to begin with a bus tour that will orientate you and show you which sights you may like to return to. Take both the lake and harbour boat trips, and visit Deichstrasse and Speicherstadt. Fit the History Museum in as soon as possible to give you background information and take a bird's-eye-view from one of the church towers. If it is the weekend you *must* visit St Pauli by night. Art lovers should beat a path to the Kunsthalle and see what big-name exhibitions are playing on the rest of the Art Mile. If you have a full three days try to fit in an excursion to Lübeck.

LONGER: ENJOYING HAMBURG TO THE FULL

Having done everything above, broaden your horizons. Hagenbeck's Zoo isn't just for kids. See where the wealthy Hamburgers live by taking the 36 bus along the Elbchaussee to Blankenese. Visit Lübeck. If you're here in summer and the weather is good, do as the Hamburgers do, hire a bike and visit the Altstadt countryside on the other side of the Elbe.

⬤ *The Grüner + Jahr Pressehaus is one of Hamburg's media powerhouses*

Something for nothing

Hamburg is one of the wealthiest cities in Europe but you don't have to spend a fortune to enjoy it. Summer is the best season in this respect, when you can walk in the city parks, along the shore of the Elbe, and, weather permitting, even relax on the beach, all for nothing.

PARKLIFE

The largest central park is Planten un Blomen, with beautiful botanic gardens, dancing fountains and various activities (see page 102). If you want peace and quiet in midweek go a little further out to Alsterpark, on the west bank of the Aussenalster. At weekends this becomes the city's most popular park.

All museums make a charge of around €6; recommended cheap museums are the *Rickmer-Rickmers* ship and the Spice Museum.

WALK UNDER THE ELBE

The bright green-domed building next to the Landungsbrücken houses the lift to the old Elbe tunnel, inaugurated in 1911. Inside there are four elevators, large enough to carry people and vehicles 24m (79ft) below the Elbe, where two tunnels lead to Steinwerder on the south side of the river. From here there is a fine view back towards the city. The tunnel is open to pedestrians and cyclists, around the clock, every day, free of charge.

AROUND THE MICHAELISKIRCHE

It's free to visit the city's most famous church, the Michaeliskirche (see page 70), even though you have to pay a small charge to ascend the tower. Next to the church it costs you nothing to see the exterior of the beautiful little Karyenkamp, and only a small charge to look inside. At the other end of the historical and architectural spectrum are the acclaimed post-modern steel and glass warehouse-style offices of one of Germany's largest publishers, the Grüner + Jahr Pressehaus – you can't miss it, as it is a landmark which also fronts on the river at Baumwall U-Bahn. The foyer is used to hold top-quality international exhibitions free of charge, including the annual World Press Photo exhibition every April–May.

WINDOW SHOPPING

Hamburg is famous for its shopping but you don't have to spend your money, just go and visit the free exhibitions; Karstadt on Mönckebergstrasse, for example, devotes its 8th floor to free exhibitions and recently attracted 300,000 visitors to its Amber Room, a replica of the lost imperial state room in St Petersburg.

BLANKENESE

Take a wander around Hamburg's loveliest village, sit on the sands and watch the big ships sailing up and down the Elbe (see page 126).

🔵 *Michaeliskirche's tower provides a great vantage point for watching passing ships*

When it rains

It rains on average one day in every three in Hamburg, so be prepared. If the weather should decide not to be too friendly, you can always hop on a sightseeing bus and take a look at Hamburg from the top deck of a double-decker bus, or pop into one of the museums, or even visit a museum ship and spend a couple of hours looking at the exhibitions until the inclement weather decides to make space for the sun, enabling you to take a walk around the city centre or sit on the terrace of a café enjoying a coffee. You might even want to visit the animals at Hagenbeck Zoo.

The best large museums are the Hamburg History Museum (see page 69) and the Arts and Crafts Museum (see page 75). The Hamburger Kunsthalle (City Art Gallery, see page 72) would grace any metropolis, the temporary exhibitions at the Bucerius Art Forum next to the Rathaus are of international calibre as are the photography exhibitions at the Deichtorhallen (see page 74). The Speicherstadt is well worth a visit for its historical significance alone: its best general-interest attractions are the Spice Museum and the huge Model Railway at Miniatur Wunderland (see page 97). However, there's plenty more to see here including the Hamburg Dungeon (see page 97) the Speicherstadt Museum (see page 96) and the German Customs Museum (Deutsches Zollmuseum, also page 96), which is free.

Other museums and galleries that might not normally be on your itinerary but which you might consider worth a detour if it really is raining *junge Hunde* (cats and dogs, literally, 'young dogs') are the Ethnological Museum (Museum für Völkerkunde), whose exhibits reflects Hamburg's importance as a world shipping centre with 'souvenirs' from every continent (see page 104), the Altona

(Altonaer) Museum, which has a wonderful collection of figureheads from old sailing ships plus many other maritime artifacts (see page 116), the Brahms Museum (see page 77) or a tour of the Rathaus (town hall, see page 66).

Hamburg shoppers are cosseted, with many of its central shops under cover, and you don't even have to get wet walking between them, as a network of arcades and covered passageways links several together just off Jungfernstieg. Even if you're not that keen on parting with your money, many of the arcades are attractive buildings in their own right and very browseable, with a particularly good range of shops and eating establishments. You could also easily spend an hour or two in large department stores like Alsterhaus or Karstadt.

All the flavours of the world at Spicy's Würzmuseum in the Speicherstadt

On arrival

TIME DIFFERENCES

Hamburg follows Central European Time (CET). During Daylight Saving Time (end Mar–end Oct) the clocks are put ahead 1 hour. In the German summer at 12.00 noon, time at home is as follows:

Australia Eastern Standard Time 20.00, Central Standard Time 19.30, Western Standard Time 18.00

New Zealand 22.00

South Africa 12.00

UK and Republic of Ireland 11.00

USA and Canada Newfoundland Time 07.30, Atlantic Canada Time 07.00, Eastern Time 06.00, Central Time 05.00, Mountain Time 04.00, Pacific Time 03.00, Alaska 02.00.

ARRIVING

By air

Hamburg Fuhlsbüttel airport lies 8 km (5 miles) north of the city centre. It is one of the largest in Germany, modern and very well equipped, though it won't be directly linked with the city's U-Bahn (underground railway) and S-Bahn (overground light railway) network until 2007–8. Meanwhile the HVV Airport Express Bus 110 bridges this gap, making the short journey to Ohlsdorf station on the U1 and S1 lines. It runs every 10 minutes, with a 10–15 minute journey time. The stop is outside Terminal 2, adult fare is €2.40, which includes the journey onwards to the city centre. You can pay on the bus or buy your ticket from the information office at the airport in the Arrivals area. From Ohlsdorf, trains take around 10–15 minutes to reach the centre.

Depending on where in the city centre you are staying, an alternative is to take a yellow Airport Express bus, run by Jasper, which goes direct to the main railway station/Hauptbahnhof (Hbf). These leave every 15–20 minutes and the journey time is 25–30 minutes. The service runs from 05.45 until midnight from the airport to Hbf, and from Hbf to the airport from 04.40 until 21.20. The bus stop is between Terminals 1 and 2. Adult fare €5 single, €7 return fare. In the small hours night bus 606 runs from Terminal 2 to Hbf and Rathausmarkt U-Bahn station in the city centre.

There are taxi-ranks in front of Terminal 1. A ride into the city centre costs about €18–20. Most major car hire operators are represented at the airport.

Lübeck Airport (Lübeck-Blankenese) is used by some low-cost carriers. It is located 8 km (5 miles) south of Lübeck, which is 59 km (37 miles) north-east of Hamburg. This is only a small airport but has most facilities. A dedicated Ryanair bus runs from Hamburg Hbf to Lübeck Airport and back, to coincide with flights. The journey takes 75–85 minutes, €8 one-way. Bus 6 (at bus stop 5) runs to Lübeck Hbf via the town centre, with a journey time of 20–30 mins. Taxis are available from outside the terminal building and are an option if you are staying in Lübeck – journey time around 20 min, cost around €16 – though it would be very expensive to hire one to Hamburg. Car hire is available at the airport. Driving into Hamburg is not recommended for short-stay leisure visitors but if you are hiring a car consult the airport website for directions.

Hamburg Fuhlsbüttel ❶ 50 75. ⓦ www.ham.airport.de)

Lübeck-Blankenese ❶ (451) 58 30 10. ⓦ www.flughafen-luebeck.de

By rail

Trains from all over Europe run to Hamburg, terminating at the

main central station Hauptbahnhof Sud (Hbf), its satellite
Hauptbahnhof Nord or at Altona, Dammtor, Bergedorf and Harburg.
All are connected to the U-Bahn (underground railway) and S-Bahn
(overground light railway) network.

By sea
Cruise ships dock in the main harbour, within walking distance or a
short train ride of the town centre.

FINDING YOUR FEET
If you are from northern Europe or indeed from a large city
anywhere in the world, there's no culture shock in Hamburg. The
vast majority of people here are polite, friendly and extremely
accommodating to English-speaking visitors. Most young Germans
and many older ones speak very good English. Hamburg has the
cosmopolitan feel and attractions of a capital city but for the visitor
at least, few of its obvious drawbacks. The pace of life is relatively
relaxed, there is no hassle and as long as you take the usual
precautions you should have no problems with crime.

As with all ports, there is a seamier side to Hamburg and drugs
and prostitution are rife in the poorer quarters of St Pauli and St
Georg, so beware cheap accommodation in the backstreets of these
districts. The main thoroughfares, including the notorious
Reeperbahn, are generally safe but always beware of side streets;
the back of the main railway station (the Kirchenallee exit) attracts
various undesirables, so don't hang around here after dark.

ORIENTATION
In the absence of a cathedral the Rathaus (town hall) is the city's
central landmark. This and the Binnenalster (the Inner Alster lake)

mark the *de facto* city centre. Two streets that you will probably find yourself returning to are Jungfernstieg ,which runs along the front of the Binnenalster, and Mönckebergstrasse, the main shopping street, which runs from the Rathausplatz (town hall square) towards the railway station. There's not much signposting for pedestrians but locals are friendly and will always help with directions – even stopping and volunteering to help if they see you poring over a map in the street.

The other main centre of activity is the docks, most easily reached by taking a U-Bahn or S-Bahn to Baumwall or Landungsbrücken. Both of these stations are on an elevated part of

IF YOU GET LOST, TRY …

Excuse me, do you speak English?
Entschuldigen Sie, sprechen Sie Englisch?
Entshuldigen zee, shprekhen zee english?

Excuse me, is this the right way to the old town/the city centre/the tourist office/ the station/the bus station?
Entschuldigung, geht es hier zur Altstadt/zur Stadtmitte/zur Touristeninformation/zum Bahnhof/zum Busbahnhof?
Entshuldeegoong, gayt es here tsoor altshtat/tsoor shtatmitter/zur Touristeninformation/tsoom baanhof/tsoom busbaanhof?

Can you point to it on my map?
Können Sie es mir bitte auf der Karte zeigen?
Kernen see es meer bitter owf der kaarte tsygen?

Haller- Str.

Rothenbaumchausee

Haller- Str.

Airport
Museum für
Völkerkunde
ROTHERBAUM

Alster-
park

Planet-
arium

Harvestehuder Weg

Herbert-Weichmann-Str.

Hofweg

Schwanenwik

Universität

E. Siemers- Alee

Mittelweg

Alsterufer

Aussenalster

ten un
nen

burger Str.

ade Fair
entre

Gorch-Fock Wal

Musikhalle

Esplanade

Kennedybrücke

Lombardsbrücke

An der Alster

Lange Reihe

Baracastr.

ST GEORG

Glockengießer Wal

E.-Merck-Str.

Binnenalster

Jungfernstieg

Steindamm

ℹ Hauptbahnhof

Adenauer Allee

Rathaus

Monckeberg strasse

Kurt-Schumacher-Allee

g Erhard Str.

Dom- Str. Spe rsort

Steinstr.

Ost-West- Str.

Nikolaifleet

Kajen B.d.Neuen B.d Mühren Zip elhaus Dovenfleet

tzen

Brooktorkal

Oberbaumbr.

Am Sandtorkal

Baumwall

Speicherstadt

HAFENCITY

Versmannstr.

e

the network and offer excellent views across the port area helping you to get your bearings. The Reeperbahn, St Pauli's main street, is just a 5-minute walk from here.

GETTING AROUND

The HVV (Hamburg Transport Association) became the world's first public transport association in 1965 and continues to run an excellent integrated system combining rapid transit rail (U-, S- and A-Bahn trains), regional rail (R-Bahn trains), bus services and even harbour ferries.

The U-Bahn and S-Bahn network makes easy work of getting around the centre and outskirts of town. As with the London Underground network, each line is designated by a colour and number. Clear signposting, indicator boards on the platform and on-board announcements make sure you know in which direction you are moving and what the next stop is. The same is true for the bus service, which fills in the gaps left by the rail services and is most useful for short hops, e.g. along the main shopping streets, or when you want to see a bit of the scenery, such as on Bus 36 to Blankenese (see page 126).

Tickets

Tickets for the U-Bahn, S-Bahn and all regional trains must be purchased in advance. The system relies on an honesty basis with no ticket barriers and few inspectors, However if you are caught without a ticket you will be fined heavily. You can buy individual tickets per journey, starting at €1.05 and increasing as you pass through more zones, but if you are around for a day or more it is worth investing in one of the passes listed opposite. Group tickets and family tickets (under 6s do not need a ticket and travel free of

charge on the HVV network) are also available on all the above.
Further information: ☎ 300 51 300. ⓦ www.hvv.de

All Day ticket The central area starts at €5.50, valid for unlimited
travel by 1 adult and 3 children under the age of 15 from the time of
purchase on the date of issue until expiry at 06.00 on the following
day. The **9AM Day Card** offers the same but is only valid after 09.00;
cost is €4.65.

Three-day ticket Valid for unlimited travel by 1 person throughout
the Greater Hamburg Area, €13.30. This ticket is transferable.

Hamburg Card This may be the best value of all. It gives unlimited
first-class travel on all public transport in the Greater Hamburg area
and also grants you free or reduced-price admission to many
attractions and excursions, including the Rathaus, St Michael's Church
and sightseeing trips around the city, the port, on the River Alster and
the lakes. You will be given a brochure with the card which details all
participating outlets and shows exactly how much you save.

🔺 *Public transport on the water, Hamburg style*

Hagenbecks Tierpark

EIMSBÜTTEL

Bundes Str.

Weiden Allee

Kleiner Beim S

Schröde

Alsenstr.

Sternschanzen park

Altonaer Str.

SCHANZEN

Stresemannstr.

Schanzen- Str.

Harkort Str.

Max-Brauer-Allee

Neuer Kamp

Fel

U

Julius-Leber Str.

Budapester Str.

Gladis C

Holstenstr.

ST PAULI

ALTONA

Re perbahn

Königstr.

Pepermöhlenbek

Heigländer Allee

Palmaille

Breite Str.

St Pauli Fischmarkt

Landungsbrücken

STEINWERDER

0   500m

N

A 1-day Hamburg Card costs €7.30, a 3-day card is €15 and is valid for 1 adult and 3 children up to the age of 14 years. You *must* sign and date it before use, otherwise it will not be valid. The Hamburg Card can be purchased at any Hamburg tourist office (see page 153).

Taxis

Taxis may be hailed on the street when the sign on the roof is illuminated. Journeys within the city are metered, journeys outside are negotiable. Rates are comparable to other northern European cities.

CAR HIRE

Driving into Hamburg has all the drawbacks of driving and parking as in any other major city and is not recommended. If you are hiring a car consult the airport website (Ⓦ www.ham.airport.de or Ⓦ www.flughaten-luebeck.de) for directions. Note that you can leave your car free of charge at one of the HVV park-and-ride facilities (see Ⓦ www.hvv.de for more information) at rapid transit and regional rail stations, which avoids the hassle of inner-city driving and parking.

Car hire operators at Hamburg airport include:

Avis ⓣ 50 75 23 14. Ⓦ www.avis.com

Budget ⓣ 50 75 38 11. Ⓦ www.budget.com

Europcar ⓣ 50 02 17 0. Ⓦ www.europcar.com

Hertz ⓣ 59 35 13 67. Ⓦ www.hertz.com

National Car Rental/ Alamo ⓣ 50 75 23 01. Ⓦ www.nationalcar.com or www.alamo.com

Sixt Affiliated to German Wings, whose passengers should book through the German Wings website to obtain a discount. ⓣ (1805) 26 25 25. Ⓦ www.e-sixt.com

Ⓞ *The view from the Michaeliskirche offers great panoramas of the city*

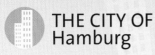

The city centre

Most of Hamburg's historical centre was burned down in two dreadful conflagrations, the great fire of 1842 which destroyed a quarter of the city centre, then in July 1943 it suffered unimaginable horror when it became the first city in the world to suffer a firestorm, at the hands of Allied bombing (see page 68). Consequently what you will see today is mostly modern with only a few surviving churches and ancient houses spared the flames and other ravages of times. It's not unattractive, however, with some striking modern buildings cheek by jowl with neo-classical facades (some new, some re-created, some restored) and a good sense of space.

Virtually nothing remains of the old city walls but the lines are still clearly marked on the map by the ring road that encircles the city centre from Holstenwall and Gorch-Fock Wall form the western boundary, running into the Lombardsbrücke, which divides the Binnenalster (inner lake) from the Aussenalster (outer lake). It is from here that the classic picture postcard photographs of the city are taken. Glockengiesserwall swings south-east past the main railway station (Hauptbahnhof) becoming Steintorwall and Klosterwall. At Deichtorplatz, just before Klosterwall can reach the docks, Ost-West Strasse slices, as the name suggest, due east–west, at right angles across it, providing a neat north–south dividing line (for the purposes of this guide at least). The city centre covered in this chapter is the area to the north of here.

SIGHTS & ATTRACTIONS

Alster lake
Most major European cities have a special square or piazza; Hamburg

Lange Reihe Barcastr.

An der Alster

Aussenalster

Adenauer Allee

Hauptbahnhof

Museum für Kunst und Gewerbe

Kurt-Schumacher-Allee

Chilehaus & Kontorhäuser

Deichtorhallen

Deichtorplatz

Kunsthalle

E-Merck-Str.

Glockengießer wal

Spitalerstraße

Mönckebergstraße

St Jacobi

St Jacobi

Steinstr.

Oberbaumbrücke

Kennedybrücke

Binnenalster

Lombardsbrücke

Boat tours

Alsterarkaden

Rathaus

Bucerius-Kunst-Forum

Spe rsort

Ost-West-Str.

Dovenfleet

Mühlenbrücke

Brooktorkai

Alst

Esplanade

Jungfernstieg

Grosse Bleichen

Neuer Wall

Alsterfleet

Dom-Str.

Ost-West-Str.

St Nikolai

Rathaus zu Mühlen B.d. Neuen B.d. Mühlen B.d.

Kajen B.d. Neuen B.d. Mühlen B.d.

Gorch-Fock Wal

Gross Neumakt

Ludwig Erhard Str.

Kramer-Witwen-Wohnung

500m

Vorsetzen

peterstrasse

Brahms Museum

Holstenwall

St Michaeliskirche

N

0

Feldstras e

Glacis Chausse

Hamburg History Museum

Karolinens

Helgoländer Allee

HERR HUMMEL

Wherever you go in the city centre you will come across the same curious statue again and again, of a clown-like figure with a yoke across his shoulders carrying two buckets of water. The statues are always the same, though each is painted and decorated individually in just about every conceivable way. Count them as you go; there are 100 in total. It commemorates 'Hans Hummel', real name Johann Wilhelm Bentz, born in 1787 at Grosse Drehbahn 36. Hummel was a curmudgeonly water-carrier teased by the city children and given the derisive nickname 'Hummel, Hummel' (meaning bumble bee). Because of the load he was carrying he couldn't catch the children but simply shouted 'Mors, Mors!' which in Low German means 'Arses, arses!'. For some reason this captured the Hamburg public imagination (in much the same way as televison catchphrases do now) and if you shout 'Hummel, Hummel!' in the street even today, over 200 years after Bentz died, the reaction will be predictably coarse!

– like Geneva – has a lake, divided into two distinct parts. While the smaller Binnenalster provides a neat blue concrete-flanked welcome mat to the city, the bucolic Aussenalster is its pride and joy, home to millionaires and consulates. Hamburgers flock here year round; on sunny summer days to take to the water and laze in the parks, and in winter, ice thickness permitting, to skate. It takes around 3 hours if you want to walk all the way around.

There are three main boat tours. The short lake tour, the Alster

● *Don't shout his name or you'll get a rude answer!*

Rundfahrt, takes just under 1 hour, roughly following the lake perimeter; the longer Alster-Kreuz-Fahrt harks back to the days when steamers were an important part of the public transport network and it tacks across the lake, making nine stops on a leisurely 2-hour cruise. You can make it last much longer by hopping on and hopping off, visiting the fashionable cafés and restaurants, or maybe even hiring out your own boat. A third variation is the Kanal Fahrt, which adds the canals around the docks to a lake tour, specifically those canals interwining the Speicherstadt.

If you'd like to see the city's twinkling lights reflected in the Alster take the Dämmertörn night cruise, which (tides allowing) also takes you through the illuminated Speicherstadt canals. By day romantics can take a 2-hour cruise aboard the vintage steamer St Georg, built 1876, with musical accompaniment. Both run May–late September. ⓐ Jungfernstieg. ❶ 35 74 240. ⓦ www.alstertouristik.de ❺ main tours late Mar/April–end Oct. Only the Alster Rundfahrt runs all year round; in winter rechristened the Punschfahrt, on account of the free glass of (mulled) wine served aboard. You can pay on board for the Alster Rundfahrt and Punschfahrt cruise; tickets for all cruises can also be bought at the Tourist Office. Ⓝ U-Bahn/S-Bahn: Jungfernstieg.

Alsterarkaden

The Italianate Alster arcades are a perfect place to sit outside in summer and a useful shelter in winter. These elegant colonnades shelter expensive clothes stores as well as affordable restaurants and cafés. Across the Alster fleet (canal) is a fine view of the Rathaus.

Rathaus (Town Hall)

This splendid castle-like edifice, adorned with statues and spiky pinnacles, is much younger than it looks, having been built in 1887.

They proudly claim it has 647 rooms ('more than Buckingham Palace') but if you want to see more than the vestibule (note the macabre clock above the main entrance door, with death on the coffin which strikes the hour) you'll need to join a tour. English language tours run, in theory, hourly at 15 minutes past the hour; however, if there isn't a minimum of English-speaking people who buy tickets for that tour you will be moved onto the next (German-speaking) tour. Highlights among the many opulent rooms are the Debating Chamber, where the 121 members of the city-state's parliament sit, and the magnificent Great Banquet Hall, where each chandelier weighs 1.5 tons and has 278 lights.

🅰 Rathausplatz. 🛈 428 31 20 10. 🕒 Open Mon–Thur 10.00–15.15 (last tour), Fri–Sun 10.00–13.15 (last tour). Charge for tour. Ⓤ U-Bahn: Rathaus.

St Jacobi/Jacobkirche (St James' Church)

This large Gothic hall-style church dated from the mid-14th century and was destroyed by bombing in 1944. Reconstructed in 1962, it has several points of interest that make it worth a visit. On the north wall are two excellent examples of Northern German painting. David Kindt's *The Rich Man and Death* (1662) warns against wealth resulting in pride, while Joachim Luhn's fine panorama depicts Hamburg as it looked in the late 17th century. Note the church's three carved and painted altar table screens, its fine alabaster and marble pulpit (1610) and its celebrated 1693 organ by master craftsman Arp Schnitger. You can hear it booming out every Thursday at noon. There are also regular concerts here July–early September on Tuesdays at 20.00. Tours of the church are given in English if requested on the first Thursday of the month at 16.00. If your German is up to it ask if you can use the lift to the top of the tower (not generally open to the public) to enjoy the views.

@ Steinstrasse. ☎ 30 37 370. ⓦ www.jacobus.de

🕐 Daily 07.00-18.00 Ⓜ U-Bahn: Mönckebergstrasse

St Nikolai/Nikolaikirche (St Nicholas' Church)

Before the *Hamburger Feuersturm* of 1943 (see box) this was the
fourth highest church in the world, reaching a height of 147.3 m
(483 ft). Today it remains a deliberately unreconstructed soot-
blackened ruin – a memorial to the victims of war and violence,
gegen das Vergessen (lest we forget). The exception is the steeple,
ironically used during that fateful night as a target point by Allied
bombers. Ironic too, that it was designed by the renowned British

THE DEAD CITY

'History's first mass fire began on the night of July 27, 1943, in
Hamburg – created by Allied incendiary raids. Within 20
minutes, two-thirds of the buildings within an area of 4.5
square miles were on fire. It took fewer than six hours for the
fire to completely burn an area of more than five square miles.
Damage analysts called it the "Dead City". Wind speeds were of
hurricane force; air temperatures were 400–500 degrees
Fahrenheit. Between 60,000 and 100,000 people were killed in
the attack.' (From an article on 'Firestorm Physics' in the
Bulletin of the Atomic Scientists 2005. According to the church's
own figures, around 34,000 people perished between 25 July
and 3 August 1943 during the Allied Air Forces' Operation
Gomorrha, and in total 55,000 Hamburg civilians were killed
during the whole of World War II.

architect George Gilbert Scott in 1874. It has recently been equipped with a lift that offers one of Hamburg's finest viewpoints. A small glass pyramid marks the entrance to the former undercroft, now used as an exhibition area with a video on the destruction (commentary in German only) and a harrowing exhibition of photographs showing the damage to buildings and people. A commentary sheet available in English, explains the Allies' political theory of 'Morale Bombing' and how it was decided that the main goal would be aimed at civilian morale 'in particular that of the workers in the defence industries'. It explains how Hamburg was targeted in retaliation for the bombing of Coventry and Birmingham, yet despite the dreadful scale of retribution maintains a dignified and remarkable equanimity.

ⓐ Willy-Brandt-Strasse 60. ① 37 11 25. Ⓦ www.mahnmal-st-nikolai.de
Ⓛ Open daily (tower and visitor centre) 10.30–18.30. Ⓝ U-Bahn: Rödingsmarkt or Rathaus.

Museum für Hamburgische Geschichte (Hamburg History Museum)

This is easily Hamburg's finest museum, covering just about every aspect of the city in a lively captivating manner with many large-scale exhibits and captions for all displays and objects in perfect English. Pick up a floor plan to help you navigate around its three, often confusing, floors. On the ground floor the huge model of the Temple of Solomon is very impressive. Don't miss Hamburg in the 20th century, a lively exhibition with domestic and shop reconstructions together with music and videos. On the first floor, there is a full-size reconstruction of part of a cog (a traditional sailing ship) and a similar reconstruction of the bridge of the Dampfer (Steamship) *Werner*, where you can step aboard and view how Hamburg harbour appeared in 1938. 'Medieval Hamburg' tells how pirates terrorised the port and shows pirate skulls pierced by huge nails which were then affixed to public places as a warning. The second floor features the history of the Jews in Hamburg, rooms from Deichstrasse (see page 95) and the largest model railway in Europe (on a scale 1:32). Check out the superb website before you visit and do pay a visit to the museum's excellent Café Fees (see pages 82 and 86)

ⓐ Holstenwall 24. ① 42 81 32. Ⓦ www.hamburgmuseum.de ⓛ Tues–Sat 10.00–17.00, Sun 10.00–18.00. Model railway open for 25 minutes only, on each hour, Tues–Sat 11.00, 12.00, 14.00, 15.00; Sun 11.00, 12.00, 14.00, 15.00, 16.00. Ⓝ U-Bahn: St Pauli.

Michaeliskirche area

The dockside at Baumwall is dominated by the post-modern steel and glass warehouse-style offices of Grüner + Jahr Pressehaus (see page 47), which makes a striking contrast to the landmark tower of St Michaeliskirche a short walk beyond.

Michaeliskirche (St Michael's Church)

'Michel' is a symbol of the city and has always been a landmark to homecoming sailors. The tower, 82 m (269 ft) high, has a distinctive copper covering and its clock face, measuring 8 m (26 ft) in diameter (larger than London's Big Ben), is the biggest in Germany. The current church dates from 1906–12, built in the style of the mid-18th century and rebuilt after World War II. Its round tiered baroque-style interior is very much like a concert hall, a function it fulfils regularly, and it is certainly worth being here at 12.00 (daily) when all three of its organs are played. The views from its tower over the port and city are superb. In the lower part of the tower there is an audio-visual show on the history of Hamburg (in German only) and there is an

🔵 'Michel' stands by the harbour, surrounded by modern Hamburg

exhibition in the crypt on the history of the church.
🔵 Englische Planke. 🔵 37 67 81 00. 🔵 Mon–Sat 09.00–17.30, Sun
10.30–17.30 May–Oct; Mon–Sat 10.00–16.30, Sun 10.30–16.30
Nov–Apr. Separate admission charges to tower, crypt and audio-
visual show. 🔵 S-Bahn/U-Bahn Landungsbrücken; S-Bahn:
Stadthausbrücke; U-Bahn: Baumwall or Rödingsmarkt.

Kramer-Witwen-Wohnung (Merchants' Widows' Almshouses)
Next door to St Michaeliskirche is a picturesque block of tiny

almshouses which were built in the 1670s for merchants' widows. Number 10 is open as a small museum while a restaurant (see page 87) occupies a number of other houses. The rest have been turned into shops.

ⓐ Krayenkamp 10. ❶ 37 50 19 88. 🕒 Tues–Sun 10.00–17.00. Small admission charge. Ⓝ S-Bahn/U-Bahn Landungsbrücken; S-Bahn: Stadthausbrücke; U-Bahn: Baumwall or Rödingsmarkt.

CULTURE

Kunsthalle (Art Gallery)

Hamburg's Kunsthalle is one of the finest and largest German galleries outside Berlin. It comprises three interconnected buildings and the emphasis is on German and north European works. If you have the stamina you can follow it chronologically from North German art in the 1400s all the way through to the 21st-century installation in the Galerie der Gegenwart (Gallery of Contemporary Art), housed in its own striking white modernist cube building. Beware, though, that the layout is not particularly easy to follow, even with the map leaflet *Was ist wo* ('What is where').

If you intend to view the collection chronologically start your tour at the classical main entrance, nearest the Hauptbahnhof. Among the Alte Meister (Old Masters) highlights are the works of Master Bertram of Minden (Germany's first accomplished master painter known by name), Lucas Cranach, Rembrandt, Claude Lorrain and Peter Paul Rubens. German artists come to the fore in the 19. *Jahrhundert* (19th century) section, with some striking works by Caspar David Friedrichs and Phillip Otto Runge. Also in this section

🔘 *The almshouses for merchants' widows belong to another era*

are instantly recognisable French impressionist works by Manet, Monet, Renoir and co. A small 20th-century section includes works by Kokoschka and Klee.

It's a good idea to take a break at this point in the lovely Café Liebermann (see page 82), something of an artwork in itself. At this point you can either take the stairs to the Hubertus-Wald-Forum, which is devoted to temporary exhibitions excluding contemporary art, or head to the Gallery of Contemporary Art, whose remit begins in the 1960s, and also begins on the bottom floor with its main temporary exhibitions. These often feature artists of a high international reputation.

There are a further four floors of contemporary art, including a large collection of American Pop Art (Andy Warhol, Robert Rauschenberg et al.) alongside works by the most famous German contemporary artist, Joseph Beuys. The rest of the gallery space is devoted to temporary exhibitions, which invariably include multi-media installations. This gallery also has a good café.
ⓐ Glockengiesserwall. ❶ 428 131 200. ⓦ www.hamburger-kunsthalle.de ⓛ Tues–Sun 10.00–18.00, Thur 10.00–21.00. Admission charge; reduced price for 'The Blue Hour' the last hour before museum closing time (excludes Hubertus-Wald-Forum).
ⓝ U-Bahn/S-Bahn: Hauptbahnhof.

Deichtorhallen

The impressive iron-and-glass halls of the old wholesale flower market, built 1911–14, are now devoted to photography. There is a permanent collection, the Sammlung F C Gundlach, which comprises works from the fields of documentary and fashion photography as well as photographic works by fine artists and temporary exhibitions of international standing.

THE CITY CENTRE

ⓐ Deichtorstrasse 1-2. ☎ 32 10 30. ⓦ www.deichtorhallen.de
🕒 Tues–Sun 10.00–18.00. Admission charge. Ⓝ U-Bahn: Steinstrasse.

Museum für Kunst und Gewerbe (Arts and Crafts Museum)
Housed in dozens of small rooms over four floors in an old building
that is currently undergoing major renovation, this old-fashioned
jackdaw's nest varies from the Art of the Ancient World to
temporary exhibits on contemporary subjects, for example on the
World Cup 2006. You may well find some disruption to the
permanent collection at the time of your visit. Pick up a floor plan in
English and be sure to see the Musical Instruments and the Art
Nouveau rooms.

Start on the ground floor with medieval art, represented by
bronzes, goldsmith's work and ivory objects of exquisite quality. The
Renaissance collections include some world-class bronze works and

---

THE ART MILE
The stretch of road that runs between the Deichtorhallen and
the Kunsthalle is known as the Kunstmeile, or Art Mile (see
also page 19). In addition to these two major establishments is
the Museum für Kunst und Gewerbe (Arts and Crafts Museum,
see above), set just back off the main road, and almost
opposite the Deichtorhallen are three lesser known avant-
garde art venues; the Freie Akademie der Künste
(ⓦ www.akademie-der-kuenste.de), the Kunstverein in
Hamburg (ⓦ www.kunstverein.de) and the Kunsthaus
(ⓦ www.kunsthaushamburg.de). All stage contemporary art
exhibitions; see their respective websites for more details.

tapestries and outstanding inlaid cabinets furniture and artistically made cupboards as well as beautiful scientific instruments from the Renaissance and baroque periods. Complete period rooms from Hamburg houses of the 17th–19th centuries are a highlight of this floor. Begin the first floor with the Historical Keyboards collection, which began in 1890 with an endowment of 10,000 Marks to the museum by Hans von Bülow, a friend of Johannes Brahms (see page 77). Today the museum possesses some 400 European exhibits, many made in Hamburg workshops, and about 30 instruments from other parts of the world. Some of these are demonstrated on the first Sunday of the month at 16.00.

The Ancient World collection shows works of art from the Ancient Orient, Egypt and Classical Antiquity. In a Japanese tea-house the tea ceremony is normally performed on each third weekend in the month. Each visitor is served a bowl of green tea and a Japanese sweet at the end of the ceremony, which lasts about an hour (small additional charge). Don't miss the café-restaurant Destille, also on this floor (see page 82, €2 if you only want to visit here).

The Art Nouveau/Jugendstil section goes back to the Museum's founder Justus Brinckmann, who took advantage of the World Exhibition in Paris in 1900 to begin a large collection of contemporary applied art centred on furniture and room decors (there are a number of intact interiors), wall hangings, textiles, lamps, decorative objects in glass, metal, ceramics and sculptures plus books and jewellery.

The second floor is devoted mostly to design and photography with regular special exhibitions.

ⓐ Steintorplatz. ❶ 428 54 27 32. Ⓦ www.mkg-hamburg.de
🄻 Tues–Sun 10.00–18.00, Thur 10.00–21.00. Ⓝ U-Bahn/S-Bahn: Hauptbahnhof.

Kontorhaüser

Hamburg's 'Contour Houses' are colossal sombre red-brick buildings clustered around the Burchardplatz. The most famous is the ship-like **Chilehaus**, built in 1922 in Expressionist style, taking its name from the country where its owner, Henry B Sloman, made his fortune by shipping saltpetre to Hamburg. Its neighbour the Sprinkenhof is another huge office complex, which cars can drive right into.

Bucerius-Kunst-Forum

Adjacent to the Rathaus and occupying a handsome classical building, this gallery stages four major temporary exhibitions a year, ranging from the art of the ancient world to classic modern art. During 2006–2007 the schedule is: Rodin in Germany (until 25 May 2006); Frida Kahlo (17 Jun–24 Sept); Mozart in Hamburg (29 Sept–8 Oct); Cleopatra and the Caesars (28 Oct 2006–4 Feb 2007); Masterpieces of the Hudson River School from the Wadsworth Atheneum Museum of Art (24 Feb 2007–28 May 2007).
Like many of its fellow art establishments it has a fine café.
ⓐ Rathausmarkt 2. ① 36 09 960. ⓦ www.buceriuskunstforum.de
🄻 Daily 11.00–19.00. Ⓝ U-Bahn: Rathaus.

Johannes-Brahms-Museum

Johannes Brahms was born in Hamburg in 1833 in Speckstrasse. Unfortunately the house was destroyed in 1943 and the society dedicated to the great composer decided to create a museum in neighbouring Peterstrasse, itself destroyed in 1943 but convincingly re-created to its original baroque appearance and now one of the city's loveliest streets. Among the mementos here are Brahms' letters and photographs, signatures, concert programmes, scores and sheet music. Larger exhibits include the composer's writing desk and one of his pianos. In fact Brahms spent relatively little of his adult life in his native city. He settled in Vienna in 1868 and died there in 1897. ⓐ Peterstrasse 39. ① 45 21 58. ⓦ www.brahms-hamburg.de ⓛ Tues, Thur 10.00–13.00; first and third Sun in month 11.00–14.00 Jun–Sept. Admission charge. ⓝ U-Bahn: St Pauli.

RETAIL THERAPY

The city centre is the focus for Hamburg's love affair with shopping. The main retail street is Mönckebergstrasse (Mö for short) but in the event that you can't find what you want along here, there are nine major indoor centres with varying degrees of exclusivity. A tenth is on the way, the Europa Passage, which when completed will be Europe's biggest city centre mall. The emphasis throughout is on conspicuous consumption of national and international brand names in fashion, jewellery and high-class furnishings; there are few bargains or individualistic shops here.

Mönckebergstrasse

'Mö' has something for most tastes and budgets, as personified by Karstadt, the biggest department store in town. It has a huge branch devoted solely to sport, Karstadt Sporthaus, which is Europe's biggest sports goods retailer. You can try out golf clubs and tennis rackets actually hitting balls into simulators, a wind tunnel to find out how breathable your new outdoor jacket is and an artificial mountain environment to test your new footwear. There's also a rooftop area, enclosed by a safety net, devoted to an ice skating rink

● *Mönckebergstrasse is a pedestrianised paradise for shoppers*

in winter and a multi-purpose sports field in summer, complete with a four-lane 100m tartan track, where you can try out more goods before purchasing.

Probably the best place for urban fashions is Thomas-i-Punkt. The interesting old building is an attraction in its own right, quirkily fitted with, among other things, generators from a Parisian power substation with winking light and dials. Peek & Cloppenburg is one of Hamburg's largest fashion department stores. For budget fashions try C&A. There is also a large branch of Görtz, Hamburg's best shoe shop. For tea, coffee and all associated goods try Compagnie Coloniale at Mönckebergstrasse 7.

There are several malls off Mönckebergstrasse. Drop into Levantehaus, which relies more on the quality of shops and refreshment outlets than international brand names. Running parallel to Mönckebergstrasse is Spitalerstrasse, which offers good middle-market shops including the likes of H&M, Zara and Thalia (Hamburg's largest bookshop).

On and around Jungfernstieg

The grand old retail lady of Hamburg is Alsterhaus, the city's oldest department store and something of an icon. Although it has always been prestigious it has recently been refitted and gone further upmarket. It boasts a huge cosmetics department, Hamburg's biggest wine choice and a splendid fine foods department.

Off here runs Neuer Wall, a street devoted to affluent designer label collectors with the likes of Boss, Escada, Hermes, Jil Sanders, Vercase and Joop. Unger alone has over 100 international designers (Roberto Cavalli, D&G, Diane von Furstenburg, Missoni, Hogan, Loewe, etc) under one roof. At no. 11 Ladage & Oelke is a curiosity, stocking English gentleman's outfits since 1845. The southern end of

MACCA'S FAB GEAR

Although Karstadt would no longer be the first shopping choice for hip young musicians it was here that the Beatles bought some of their clothes when in Hamburg in the 1960s. 'You could get great leather gear in Hamburg'. Paul McCartney told the newspapers. 'We went home to Liverpool wearing the clothes we had bought in Hamburg. Everyone thought we were the latest "in" group from Germany and remarked on how well we spoke English!'

the street is a mecca for high-class furnishings. There's more of the same at the stylish Hamburger Hof, a classy upmarket mall part housed in a late 19th-century building on Jungfernstieg.

In a typical Hanseatic red-brick building with soaring domes, the Hanseviertel mall is on Grosse Bleichen, off Jungfernstieg. Tom Tailor may be worth a look in, featuring good quality casual wear at affordable prices for all the family. On the opposite side of Grosse Bleichen is the Kaufmannshaus, a mall in a steel-and-glass building that is worth seeing, as is the Bleichenhof mall.

TAKING A BREAK

Although Hamburg may not have the same reputation for its café culture as, say, Italian cities or Vienna, a coffee and cake in the centre of town is invariably a treat. This is due in no small part to the large number of shops, the well-heeled clientele and the city's heritage and expertise in shipping tea and coffee. Competition means prices are usually reasonable too.

Museum and gallery cafés

Café Fees A beautiful place for a break while visiting the Museum of Hamburg History, sitting inside or out whatever the weather, as well as one of the city's most atmospheric restaurants (see 'After Dark', page 86).

Café Liebermann This charming café, named after the German Impressionist painter Max Liebermann, is set in the original 19th-century part of the Kunsthalle with tall marble columns. See page 72 for details. No charge for entrance to café only.

Destille It is worth a trip to the Arts and Crafts museum for the café alone, decorated in the style of a *Gaststube* (traditional tea parlour) around the turn of the 20th century, albeit with valuable paintings around the walls. The cold buffet of Scandinavian and German meats and dishes is excellent. See page 75 for details. Entrance to café only, small charge.

Other cafés

Alsterpavilion Highly popular on a summer's day, owing largely to its location opposite the Alsterhaus store and next to the Jungfernstieg boat stage. The quality is good, though you may have to wait to be served. ⓐ Jungfernstieg. ❶ 350 18 70. ⓛ Open daily 09.00/10.00–late (summer 01.00).

Arkaden-Café On a summer's day when the geranium-decked riverside terrace is open, this is the place to be in the centre of town, crammed with out-of-town visitors, shoppers and ladies who lunch.

◗ *Hamburg relaxes in the cafés of the Alsterarkaden*

Get there early to get a good seat. 🅐 Alsterarkaden 910. 🛈 35 76 06 30. 🕒 09.00–late.

Café Condi See how the other half lives in this lovely Biedermeier (early to mid-19th century Germanic) style café in the city's most prestigious hotel, the Raffles Vier Jahreszeiten. 🅐 Neuer Jungfernstieg 9–14. 🛈 34 94 33 15. 🝏 www.raffles-hvj.de 🕒 Mon–Sat 10.30–18.30 (breakfast 06.15–10.30), Sun breakfast only 07.15–11.30.

Die Rösterei Lively modern café useful for a shopping break at the top end of Mönckebergstrasse. 🅐 Levante Haus, Mönckebergstrasse 7. 🛈 30 39 37 35. 🕒 Daily 09.00– 21.00 (closed Sun in winter).

Grill & Green Light, airy, modern bistro-style restaurant with a terrace on the Alster canal in the basement of the Bleichenhof shopping arcade. The food is up-to-date, healthy, fresh and good value; salads, pastas, grills, wok dishes, tortillas and so on. 🅐 Bleichenbrücke 9. 🛈 35 30 50. 🕒 Mon–Sat 12.00–23.00, Sun brunch 10.30–23.00. 🝏 www.grillandgreen.de

Gourmet Station The new food court in Hauptbahnhof is not the most restful of places for a break but there is an excellent choice of

CAFÉS WITH A VIEW
The café of the Alsterhaus looks directly onto the Binnenalster from its fourth floor location; Flow Restaurant bistro at Karstadt Sport has a 5th-floor roof garden with views over the centre of town.

outlets, both in terms of styles and nationalities of food. You can get just about everything from coffee and cake to full meals from around the world. The quality of catering and service is high and the seating in many cases is very comfortable. ❸ Hauptbahnhof. ⏰ Most places open daily from 08.00–late.

Le Paquebot Set just off Mönckebergstrasse, the art deco style café-restaurant of the Thalia-Theater is an excellent spot for a light lunch or a coffee while shopping. ❸ Gerhart-Hauptmann Platz. ☎ 32 65 19. ⏰ Mon–Sat 11.00–01.00.

Ratsweinkeller More of a place for a full meal but you'll be welcome here at any time for a coffee or a beer and it's certainly worth a look if you are visiting the Ratshaus. See page 87 for details.

AFTER DARK

Most of Hamburg's nightlife takes place in the St Pauli area and elsewhere, but the city centre still offers a good choice of bars, restaurants and entertainment options.

Restaurants
Franziskaner €–€€ For a slice of good old German *gemütlichkeit* go along (preferably in a group) to try the typical Bavarian and German specialities in the friendly atmosphere of this Munich-style restaurant. ❸ Grosse Theaterstrasse 9/Colonnaden. ☎ 34 57 56. 🌐 www.restaurant-franziskaner.de ⏰ Mon–Sat 11.30–24.00. Ⓝ U-Bahn: Gänsemarkt.

Prinz & König €–€€ This attractive traditional-meets-modern pub-cum-restaurant is one of the central area's favourite bars, serving food well into the small hours. The house speciality is steak on a hot stone; the lunchtime dish of the day is terrific value. Regular live music. ⓐ Poststrasse 53. ⓣ 35 47 98. ⓦ www.prinzundkoenig.de ⓛ Mon–Sat 11.00–0.400; Sun 17.00–04.00. ⓝ U-Bahn/S-Bahn: Jungfernstieg.

Saliba €–€€ Excellent Syrian and Lebanese food is served in this cosy little candlelit restaurant in the Alsterarkaden. The mezes (hors d'oeuvres) alone are a feast. There is a larger, very popular branch in Altona. ⓐ Alsterarkaden, Neuen Wall 13. ⓣ 34 50 21. ⓦ www.saliba.de ⓛ Daily 11.00–23.00 (last orders 22.00). ⓝ U-Bahn: Rathaus.

Café Fees €€ This splendid Orangery-style building mixes Gothic fittings, ornate chandeliers, art nouveau and 21st-century style perfectly. It has a beautiful glass-covered courtyard with patio heaters for all year use. There is a short but interesting full menu of modern German dishes and this is a popular meeting place for Sunday brunch. ⓐ Gerhofstrasse 40 (Museum of Hamburg History). ⓣ 35 31 32. ⓦ www.fees-hamburg.de ⓛ Tues–Sun 10.00–02.00; Fri–Sat 10.00–04.00. Meals served 10.00–15.00 Tues–Sat, Thur–Sat 18.00–24.00. ⓝ St Pauli.

Old Commercial Room €€ A traditional Hamburg favourite next to the Michaeliskirche. The interior is nautically themed and old-fashioned and the menu is unexciting but always reliable. It is said to be the best place in town for *Labskaus* (see page 25). ⓐ Englische Planke 10. ⓣ 36 63 19. ⓦ www.oldcommercialroom.de ⓛ Daily 12.00–24.00. ⓝ U-Bahn: Rödingsmarkt.

Ratsweinkeller €€ For traditional atmosphere and surroundings and hearty local and regional dishes, the town hall wine cellar, the oldest restaurant in town, is the place to come. Try the mirror carp, *Jägertopf* (goulash with dumplings) or perhaps *Oldenburger Gänserkeule* (sweet and sour goose leg with cranberry sauce). ⓐ Entrances on Grosse Johanisstrasse and via the Rathaus. ① 36 41 53. ◑ Mon–Sat 11.00–23.00, Sun 11.00–15.30. Ⓝ U-Bahn: Rathaus.

Alt-Hamburger Aalspeicher €€–€€€ Beautiful traditional restaurant in one of Deichstrasse's 17th-century houses, specialising in traditional Hamburg fish dishes. Ask for a window seat to enjoy the views over the Nikolaifleet back towards town. ⓐ Deichstrasse 43. ① 36 29 90. Ⓦ www.aalspeicher.de ◑ Daily 12.00–24.00. Ⓝ U-Bahn: Rödingsmarkt.

Krameramtstuben am Michel €€–€€€ Entering this almost hidden world of tiny almshouses (see page 71) is a little bit like stepping into a period film set, or even a giant doll's house, and the authentic local cooking makes this a quintessential old-world Hamburg experience. There are lots of different rooms so look around if you are given the choice. ⓐ Krayenkamp 10. ① 36 58 00. Ⓦ www.krameramtsstuben.de ◑ Daily 12 .00–24.00. Ⓝ U-Bahn: Rödingsmarkt.

Tsao Tang €€–€€€ This very stylish but relaxed Chinese restaurant offers genuine Chinese cuisine from Canton, Szechuan and Peking and is frequented by Chinese locals and business people. Dim sum is served in the evening and the speciality is Peking-style roast duck. The service is impeccable. ⓐ Hotel Kempinski Grand Atlantic.

❶ 28 00 41 88. ⏱ Daily 12.00–15.00, 18.00–23.30. Ⓝ U-Bahn/S-Bahn: Hauptbahnhof.

Plat du Jour €€€ Fine French bistro cooking aimed at the business community is on offer at this long-established Hamburg favourite but the eponymous plat du jour provides good value for budget-conscious visitors too. ⓐ Dornbusch 4. ❶ 32 14 14. ⏱ Mon–Sat 12.00–22.30. Ⓝ U-Bahn: Rathaus.

Entertainment
Cotton Club Established in 1959, the Cotton Club stages live jazz and occasional blues with the emphasis on Dixieland hot jazz and swing. Smokey pub atmosphere, reasonable prices. ⓐ Alter Steinweg 10. ❶ 34 38 78. ⓦ www.cotton-club.org ⏱ Mon–Sat doors open 20.00, music 20.30. Ⓝ S-Bahn: Stadthausbrücke; U-Bahn: Rödingsmarkt.

Hamburgische Staatsoper The Hamburg State Opera is ranked among the very best in the world and its ballet company has a high reputation, too. The Hamburg Philharmonic State Orchestra provide the music for most opera and ballet productions.
ⓐ Dammtorstrasse. ❶ 40 35 68 68. ⓦ www.hamburgische-staatsoper.de Ⓝ U-Bahn: Stephansplatz.

Bars
Bar Hamburg The haunt of the beautiful people and some of the best DJs in Hamburg, Jazz, house and lounge music to sip your cocktails (a choice of over 250) and nibble your sashimi by.
ⓐ Rautenbergstrasse 6–8. ❶ 28 05 48 80. ⓦ www.barhamburg.com
⏱ Daily 19.00–late. Ⓝ U-Bahn/S-Bahn: Hauptbahnhof.

GOOD AREAS FOR BARS

The best area in the city centre for a bar crawl is Grossneumarkt (Ⓢ S-Bahn: Stadthausbrücke), where you'll also find a good choice of informal eating places. On summer nights the square is packed. Try Schwenders if you want an elegant café restaurant or Thämers for a cosy pub-style bar. Another popular area is Lange Reihe in the St Georg district, next to Hauptbahnhof. Café Gnosa at no. 93 has an interesting 1950s interior and caters for a mixed straight and gay crowd. Two good places to eat on Lange Reihe are Turnhalle (no. 107) – for bistro food and Cox (no. 68), part of the Hamburg's *Szene-Treffs* (fashionable meeting places) for new German cooking.

Max und Consorten A very popular down-to-earth bar, with a mixed crowd of visitors and locals spanning the age spectrum, where Bier und Wurst are the staple refreshment option. Ⓐ Spadenteich 7. Ⓣ 24 56 17. Ⓛ Daily 10.00–late. Ⓝ U-Bahn/S-Bahn: Hauptbahnhof.

Zum Brandanfang Very *gemütlich*, attractive, friendly little pub in an historic house which goes back to 1650. Bar meals are served in the front and there is a restaurant area in the back. Ⓐ Deichstrasse 25. Ⓣ 36 55 20. Ⓛ Daily 11.00–23.00. Ⓝ U-Bahn: Rödingsmarkt.

Hamburg harbour

Although most of the city's once great shipbuilding industry has been lost to the Far East, the vast majority of goods that enter Germany today still pass through Hamburg, and as it has done for centuries, the port provide the city with its wealth. Depending on the definition of 'port', 'container port' or 'harbour', this is the largest or second largest in Europe (after Rotterdam) and employs 155,000 people. It comprises 60 basins and around 45 km (27 miles) of quays. Around 300 shipping lines call here regularly to transport goods to and from 1000 ports all over the world. The *Landungsbrücken* (landing stages) on the harbour front, which float to allow for the tides (3.5 m/11 ft on average), are the longest of their kind in the world.

During World War II the harbour area was a key Allied target and very few buildings survived the bombing. The Speicherstadt (literally, 'warehouse town'), however, retains its history and there are a couple of notable small 17th-century enclaves in this area.

The U-Bahn runs along the harbour front on an elevated section of track between Baumwall and Landungsbrücken stations and is useful for continuing on to St Pauli and Reeperbahn stations, which service the Reeperbahn, St Pauli's main street.

SIGHTS & ATTRACTIONS

Hafenrundfahrten (Harbour tours)

There are three kinds of tour: around the harbour, around the canals of the Speicherstadt or a combination of the two. Just the harbour or just the canals take around an hour. There is only one regular English-language harbour tour available to the general public (i.e.

without a group booking). This leaves daily at noon, March to November, from the Landungsbrücken, Brücke (pier) 1 (☎ 31 78 22 31).

Some single-deckers cruisers combine the harbour and the canals, though these are not as comfortable as the larger ships and few offer English-language commentaries. One that does occasional tours in English is Elbe-und Hafentouristik Glitscher at Brücke 6, 7 (☎ 737 4343; ⊛ www.glitscher-hamburg.de). You can buy tickets for all harbour cruises at the tourist office and ask them about English-language tours.

Rickmer Rickmers

Named after the son of the owner – his cherubic face smiles down from the ship's figurehead – this former East Indies windjammer dates from 1896, and was one of the last three-masted sailing ships to be built in Germany. The *Rickmer Rickmers* sailed the oceans of the world for 66 years and could carry loads of up to 3000 tons with a crew of just 24, who would be away from shore for up to five months at a time. It is now a museum; areas open to visitors includes the engine room, the crew's quarters and galleys, and there are special exhibitions. The ship is also home to an attractive restaurant.

🖈 Ponton 1A, Landungsbrücken. ☎ 319 59 59. ⊛ www.rickmer-rickmers.de 🕐 Daily 10.00–18.00. Admission charge.
Ⓜ U-Bahn/S-Bahn: Landungsbrücken.

Cap San Diego

The world's largest seaworthy museum ship, built in 1961, measures almost 160 m (525 ft) long and weighs 6700 tons. There is nothing particularly remarkable about this freighter until you descend into

▶ *Herr Rickmers' son stares out from his father's ship*

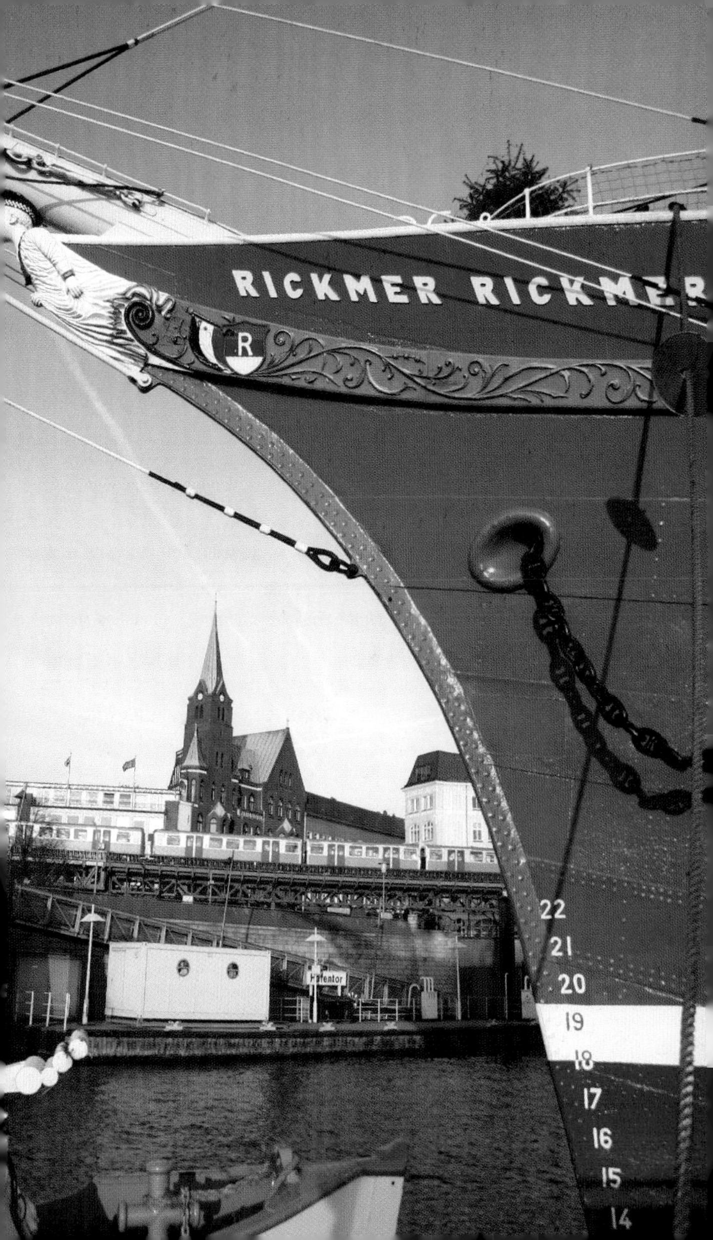
RICKMER RICKMER
R
Hafentor
22
21
20
19
18
17
16
15
14

the engine room. Deep in the ship's bowels the size and complexity of the machinery will awe even the most technically challenged of visitors.

The other highlight is the exhibition A *Suitcase Packed with Hope*, which documents how, between 1836 and 1914, 5 million people used Hamburg as a departure point from Europe. Huge evocative black and white photographs and memorabilia show the often deplorable early conditions which the emigrants had to suffer but how, too, the Hamburg authorities built a whole new suburb to accommodate them and ease their way (English captions). If the exhibition does not put you off the idea, you can spend the night on board, in a very comfortable cabin (€80 double cabin).

ⓐ Überseebrücke. ☎ 36 42 09. ⓦ www.capsandiego.de
🕒 Daily 10.00-18.00. Admission charge. Ⓝ U-Bahn: Baumwall.

More ships

There are two other unusual and very contrasting vessels open to the public in the Hamburg docks. The bright red **Lightship**, next to the *Cap San Diego*, now functions mainly as a floating restaurant and café (see page 99) and is also a great little jazz venue.

The most intriguing ship of all, **U-434**, a huge 90 m (295 ft) long Russian submarine from the Cold War era, is a little way from here in a relatively remote part of the docks.

ⓐ Versmannstrasse. ☎ 32 00 49 34. ⓦ www.u-434.de 🕒 Mon–Thur 10.00–18.00, Fri–Sun and hols 09.00–19.00 Apr–Sept; daily 10.00–18.00 Oct–Mar. Admission charge. Ⓝ The red double-decker Stadtrundfahrt sightseeing bus calls here and you don't have to buy the full city tour ticket to board. Ask for a special U-434 ticket (small charge) which will get you from the Landungsbrücken to the submarine and back to the Hauptbahnhof.

Speicherstadt

The typically Hanseatic dark-red brick Speicherstadt is the biggest warehouse complex in the world, with 373,000 sq m (447,000 sq yd) of storage space housing such valuable goods as coffee, tea, tobacco, spices, alcoholic drinks, oriental carpets and silks. Under the privileges granted to the port they may be stored duty-free for as long as their owners wish before they are sold – usually when market prices rise to a sufficiently tempting price.

The Speicherstadt was built between 1855 and 1910. Around half of it was destroyed during the war but it has been subsequently restored and the buildings are protected, so even today you will see old-fashioned mechanical hoists being used, as modern lifts cannot be installed. The Speicherstadt incorporates some good museums – the Deutsches Zollmuseum, Speicherstadt Museum, Spice Museum and the Afghan Museum (see pages 96 and 97).

At the western end of the Speicherstadt (towards the harbour), the Kehrwiedersteg bridge crosses the water back towards the city into Deichstrasse. Some of the city's oldest and most picturesque buildings, dating back to the 17th century, lie along here. At the

GUIDED WALKS

The tourist board organises a number of guided walks covering the Speicherstadt: Warehouse Complex and PortCity tours depart Tuesday 16.00 (1 Apr–31 Oct) from Baumwall U-Bahn; Warehouse Complex Tours go year round Sunday 11.00 from Kornhausbrücke (no reservations required); *Warehouse Complex* and *PortCity– Blending Traditions with the Future*, departs Sunday 14.00 (Feb–Late Nov).

back of the houses is the Nikolaifleet canal, and on the other side, on the street known as Cremona, are also several ancient, photogenic houses. Several have been turned into places to eat and drink.

Deutsches Zollmuseum (German Customs Museum)

The former customs post is now a museum illustrating the difficulties of preventing theft, smuggling and counterfeit goods through the ages.

ⓐ Alter Wandrahm 16. ❶ 300 876 11. Ⓦ www.museum.zoll.de
🕒 Tues–Sun 10.00–17.00. Admission free. Ⓥ U-Bahn: Messberg.

Speicherstadt Museum

This atmospheric little display is a logical introduction to the Speicherstadt, even if the exhibits, such as typical tools and samples of goods, are workaday.

ⓐ St Annenufer 2. ❶ 32 11 91. Ⓦ www.speicherstadtmuseum.de
🕒 Tues–Sun 10.00–17.00 (also Mon on public hols). Admission charge. Ⓥ U-Bahn: Messberg.

Spicy's Gewürzmuseum

'The hottest admission ticket in town' (a packet of black peppercorns, which you get to keep as your entrance receipt) sets the tone for this very likeable trawl through the world of spices. All captions are in perfect English, your knowledge is tested en route and perhaps most enjoyable of all are the many old-fashioned examples of packaging and advertising memorabilia and curiosities from around the world, such as the model ship from Indonesia made entirely from cloves.

ⓐ Am Sandtorkai 32. ❶ 36 79 89. Ⓦ www.spicys.de 🕒 Tues–Sun 10.00–17.00. Admission charge. Ⓥ U-Bahn: Baumwall.

Afghanisches Kunst und Kulturmuseum (Museum of Afghan Art & Culture)

A small but very colourful introduction to the country which has supplied so many exotic goods (especially carpets and spices) to the Speicherstadt.

Ⓐ Am Sandtorkai 32/1. ☎ 37 82 36. Ⓦ www.afghanisches-museum.de
🕐 Daily 10.00–17.00. Admission charge. Ⓤ U-Bahn: Baumwall.

HafenCity

In the empty docklands area that lies roughly behind the attractions listed above (from Wandrahmbrücke to Kehrwiederspitze) a whole new 'Harbour City' is taking shape which will be the biggest project of its kind in Europe. A former boiler house, the Kesselhaus, has been renovated and converted into the HafenCity InfoCenter, featuring a large scale-model and various exhibits. Admission is free and it has a good café.

Ⓐ Am Sandtorkai 30. ☎ 36 90 17 99. Ⓦ www.HafenCity.com
🕐 Tues–Sun 10.00–18.00. Admission free. Ⓤ U-Bahn: Baumwall.

Hamburg Dungeon

Hamburg's horrible history is depicted here in all its gruesome gore, including the execution of the feared pirate Störtebeker and 70 of his companions, and death and destruction in the Great Fire of Hamburg. Not for the fainthearted or young children but teens love it.

Ⓐ Kehrwieder 2. ☎ 36 00 55 20. Ⓦ www.hamburgdungeon.com
🕐 Daily 11.00–18.00. Admission charge. Ⓤ U-Bahn: Baumwall.

Miniatur Wunderland

This is the largest H0-size model railroad layout in the world, comprising more than 1000 trains hauling over 15,000 carriages around models of Hamburg, Scandinavia, the Florida Keys and lots more national and international mini-landscapes. You can be part of the action, pushing buttons so that a mine train starts, a shark chases a diver, 'GOAL!!!' sounds from the Hamburg AOL football stadium, and so on. Every few minutes the main lights dim, and around 200,000 tiny bulbs illuminate this engaging little world.

ⓐ Kehrwieder 2. ⓣ 36 09 11 57. ⓦ www.miniatur-wunderland.de ⓛ Mon, Wed–Fri 10.00–18.00, Tues 10.00–21.00, Sat, Sun & holidays 09.00–20.00. Admission charge. ⓝ U-Bahn: Baumwall.

Die Dachbodenbande (Toy Museum)

Two hundred years' worth of toys are the theme of this charming little museum.

ⓐ Kehrwieder 4. ⓣ 0172 329 3250. ⓦ www.dachbodenbande.de ⓛ Daily 10.00–18.00. Admission charge. ⓝ U-Bahn: Baumwall.

Rahimi Trading

Rahimi specialise in importing and wholesaling oriental carpets but also deal with goods from all over the East, including furniture, china porcelain, mirrors and pictures which they sell direct to the public in a warehouse space that looks like something from The 1001 Nights.

ⓐ Am Sandtorkai 32. ⓣ 36 47 19. ⓛ Mon–Fri 09.00–17.00; Sat–Sun by appt 11.00–16.00. ⓝ U-Bahn: Baumwall.

TAKING A BREAK

Many of the little *Kajüte* (cabins) on the Landungsbrücken serve good quality fish rolls to take away or eat in, as well as inexpensive fish meals.

Café im Kesselhaus Simple but stylish café specialising in hearty soups, good wholefood snacks and salads – ideal when visiting the Speicherstadt, where there are few refreshment options.
ⓐ Am Sandtorkai 30. ⓣ 36 90 17 99. ⓛ Tues–Sun 10.00–18.00.
Ⓝ U-Bahn: Baumwall.

Feuerschiff (Lightship) It's worth popping on board if only to see inside this bright red lighthouse ship (built in England as a fireship) and you can enjoy a coffee, a beer, a snack or a full meal at any time of the day. It is at its best, however, on Sunday lunchtime or Monday evening, when a jazz band plays. The busy low-ceilinged interior, with its multi-levels, makes a perfect setting and there's a friendly lively atmosphere. ⓐ City Sporthafen. ⓣ 36 25 53.
ⓦ www.das-feuerschiff.de ⓛ Bar: Mon–Sat 11.00–13.00, Sun 10.00–22.30. Restaurant: Mon–Sat 12.00–22.00, Sun 10.00–17.00. Jazz: Sun 11.00–14.40, Mon from 20.30 onwards. Admission charge for jazz sessions. Ⓝ U-Bahn: Baumwall.

Beach clubs
In the chill of midwinter it's hard to believe this is possible and even in season there's something a little bit tongue-in-cheek about the whole thing, but from 1 May to the mid/end September beach life is re-created (as far as that is possible when it is 15°C (59°F) and raining outside) on the banks of the Elbe by a number of 'beach clubs'. Colonial furniture, decking, deck chairs, potted palms, chill-out music, tropical cocktails, barbecues, even beach volleyball on brought-in white sand, all helps creates the illusion of exotic climes. The nearest one to town is StrandPauli (ⓦ www.strandpauli.de), in between the Landungsbrücken and the Fischmarkt. A little further downriver are Hamburg City Beach Club, (ⓦ www.hamburgcitybeachclub.de), Lago

Bay (🅦 www.lago.cc) and Hamburg del Mar (🅦 www.hamburg-del-mar.de). The latter even organise a Christmas beach club on the Alster!

AFTER DARK

The Tower Bar Located right on top of the landmark Hafen Hotel, this offers easily the best view of the area by night, with the port to one side and the spectacular lights of the Dom funfair (when it is there) to the other. Start your night off here with a Happy Hour drink. 🅐 Seewartenstrasse 9. 🅣 31 11 30. 🅛 Daily 18.00–02.00 (Happy Hour 18.00–19.00). 🅝 U-Bahn/S-Bahn: Landungsbrücke.

Gröninger Braukeller & Brauhaus Hanseat Dehns Privatbrauerei This Braukeller in the south of the old town has been brewing on the premises since 1750. A good-time bar with *Wurst* und *Kartoffeln* (sausage and potatoes) to soak up the copious quantities of home-brewed beer that is drunk here. Go with a group to get the best out of it. 🅐 Ost-West-Strasse 47. 🅣 33 13 81. 🅛 Mon–Fri 11.00–late, Sat 17.00–late. 🅝 U-Bahn: Messberg.

Kehrwieder Varieté-Musik-Theater Although the Kehrwieder theatre bills itself as cabaret, its repertoire usually includes airborne and stage acrobatics plus clowns, jugglers, music and dance routines, so the sheer spectacle and its splendid setting in the Speicherstadt may well outweighs any difficulties with the language. You can also eat here at a reasonable price. 🅐 Kehrwieder 6. 🅣 31 18 64 02. 🅦 www.kehrwieder-variete.de

▶ *The Lightship is an unmissable sight on Hamburg's waterfront*

North of the centre

Aside from visiting the Aussenalster lake, most short-stay visitors to Hamburg don't venture north of the old city wall boundary – which is a shame, particularly in good weather, because just beyond is the lovely northern section of the Planten un Blomen gardens, one of the world's best zoos, and around the lakeside, beautiful parkland with cafés and restaurants frequented by well-heeled locals at the weekend.

For the location of places mentioned in this chapter, see the main city map, pages 54–55.

SIGHTS & ATTRACTIONS

Planten un Blomen
The largest city park, Planten un Blomen is part of a green belt that stretches north from the St Pauli U-Bahn station and the Hamburg History Museum (see page 69) as far as the Fernsehturm (see page 105). The southern section includes a children's adventure playground, mini-golf and trampolines, a roller-skating rink (converted to ice-skating in winter) and a 'water-playground'. The northern half is more decorative though it too includes a large play area for children and pony rides. Adults are more likely to enjoy the Planten un Blumen, botanical gardens including an apothecaries' garden, a rose garden, a tropical greenhouse and Europe's largest Japanese Garden. This includes a tea house where special exhibitions on aspects of Oriental culture are held and the tea ceremony is demonstrated. Also in the northern section on summer

◗ *Planten un Blomen is Hamburg's green heart*

> **HERE ON BUSINESS?**
>
> Then you may well be heading to the Planten un Blomen park which is home to not only Hamburg's largest trade fairs and conventions centre, the Messe Hallen, but also the Hamburg Messe und Congress (Congress Zentrum Hamburg). This is one of the largest congress centres in the world, with seating for up to 10,000 delegates.

nights fountains illuminated by coloured lights dance in the lake and there are concerts of classical and jazz music.

Ⓦ www.plantenunblomen.hamburg.de. Ⓛ Daily. 07.00–23.00 May–Sept; 07.00–20.00 Oct–Apr. Illuminated fountains and concerts: 22.00 May–Aug; 21.00 Sept. Tea House: Tues–Sat 15.00–18.00 May–Sept. The dancing fountains are also switched on daily for 'performances' at 14.00, 16.00, 18.00; on Sundays and holidays recorded music is added to the 14.00 performance. Tropical greenhouse: Mon–Fri 09.00–16.45, Sat–Sun 10.00–17.45 Mar–Oct; Mon–Fri 09.00–15.45, Sat–Sun 10.00–15.45 Nov–Feb. Admission free to all areas except mini-golf and trampolines. Ⓝ U-Bahn: Dammtor, Stephansplatz, St Pauli or Messehallen.

Alsterpark

The city's most popular park, on the west bank of the Aussenalster, is a lovely spot for a walk and a picnic by the lake (see page 27).
Ⓝ U-Bahn: Hallerstrasse

Museum für Völkerkunde (Ethnological Museum)

Hamburg's most exotic museum is a treasure chest of souvenirs collected by merchants and seafarers from Africa, Asia, America, Oceania and the more far-flung corners of Europe, ever since its inception in 1879. These range in size from moccasins from North America to a full-scale Maori Meeting Hall. The masks from Oceania are a favourite.

❸ Rothenbaumchaussee 64. ❶ (01805) 30 88 88.
Ⓦ www.voelkerkundemuseum.com Ⓛ Tues–Sun 10.00–18.00, Thur 10.00–21.00. Admission charge. Ⓝ U-Bahn: Hallerstrasse; S-Bahn: Dammtor.

Fernsehturm (Television Tower)

Hamburg's tallest structure, at nearly 280 m (919 ft) high, was until recently open to the general public, who came to enjoy its revolving restaurant and viewing platform. A hardy few even made bungee jumps from here. Sadly it is now closed to the public. Ⓝ U-Bahn: Messehallen.

Hagenbecks Tierpark (Hagenbecks Zoo)

Established in 1907, Hagenbecks is one of the world's leading zoos and pioneered the principle of keeping animals in near-natural enclosures without cages. Today it is home to around 2500 animals representing 360 species, many of which are housed in the 56 open-air spaces. The park is beautifully landscaped with lakes and crags and botanical gardens with rare plants. In the Troparium (an aquarium-cum-terrarium) you can experience the underwater world of the tropical seas as well as small animals from the jungle and the deserts.

Young children are particularly well catered for with an excellent playground, a popular train ride and pony rides. Hagenbecks is also one of the few zoos in Europe that still offers elephant rides. In the

● *You can still ride an elephant at Hagenbecks*

children's zoo are pygmy and Ovambo goats, and giraffes and
elephants may also be fed, as long as they're offered fresh fruits or
vegetables.

In summer the zoo stages a series of special evenings on some
Saturday nights (small additional charge). Jungle Nights, featuring
exotic music and entertainment, runs from mid-May to early June,
while Romantic Nights in August brings live classical music.

ⓐ Lokstedter Grenzstrasse 2. ① 540 00 10. ⓦ www.hagenbeck.de
ⓛ Daily. 09.00–17.00 (19.00 if weather permits) mid-Mar–Oct;
09.00–16.30 Nov–mid-Mar. Admission charge.
ⓝ U-Bahn: Hagenbecks Tierpark.

Planetarium Hamburg

Located just beyond the northern tip of the Aussenalster in the Stadtpark, one of the most advanced planetariums in the world. The commentary is only in German but you won't need words to appreciate the state-of-the-art cosmos simulator, Digistar 3, which takes visitors on a three-dimensional journey over millions of light years in 'Eternal Worlds – from the Big Bang to planet Earth', witnessing the life and death of stars and galaxies.

While you are waiting for the show there's a window on the universe via large format high-resolution plasma screens linked online to the Hubble Space Telescope. If you want more down-to-earth views after all that, step up to the Observation Deck, which at a mere 50 m (164 ft) offers a fine panorama of the city with the Aussenalster in the foreground.

Music fans might also like to check out the Planetarium programme, which features special shows such as: 'Dark Side of The Moon', to the eponymous Pink Floyd album soundtrack; 'The Cosmic Wall – a monument to Pink Floyd'; 'Aero' by Jean Michel Jarre; and 'Deep Space Night', which mixes classical, pop, rock and trance music. Live concerts and laser shows are also staged here.

Ⓐ Hindenburgstrasse, Stadtpark. ☎ 428 86 52 10.
Ⓦ www.planetarium-hamburg.de 🕐 Tues 09.00–15.00, Wed 09.00–21.00, Thur 09.00–21.30, Fri 09.00–21.45, Sat 12.30–21.30, Sun 12.30–19.00. Admission charge. Ⓜ U-Bahn: Kellinghusenstrasse.

RETAIL THERAPY

This is not an area for shopping. However, head to Karolinenviertel and Schanzenviertel, between Sternschanze and Feldstrasse U-Bahn stops, and you will find attractive designer stores.

TAKING A BREAK

Bodo's Bootssteg A Hamburg legend and one of the nicest places
for a break on the Aussenalster, where you can have a coffee in the
lovely Alsterpark (see page 104) while sitting in a lounger watching
the yachts go by. Harveste-huder Weg 1b. 410 35 25. Daily
11.00–late in summer; Sat–Sun from 11.00 in winter. U-Bahn:
Klosterstern.

Café Schöne Aussichten In the northern section of the Planten un
Blomen park this café lives up to its name, with 'beautiful views'
from its shady terrace. It is very popular in summer and serves until
late into the evening to the sounds of house and soul music.
 Gorch-Fock Wall 1. 34 01 13. Sun–Thur 10.00–24.00; Fri–Sat
10.00–02.00. Free admission. Thur after 18.00, After Work Club (see
opposite), admission charge. S-Bahn:Dammtor.

Sommer Terrassen The Summer Terrace is a little way out of the
centre but if you want to experience a real beer garden in a leafy
park choose a nice warm summer night and head here; ideal for
after visiting the Planetarium. Südring 44, south side of
Stadtpark. 27 06 274. U-Bahn: Borgweg.

AFTER DARK

Hamburg University is located immediately north of the Planten un
Blomen gardens and its presence ensures a number of lively bars in
the area; Grindelallee in particular is heaving with cafés. For the best
nightlife, however, you'll have to go immediately west to the
Schanzen district (Schanzenviertel), between St Pauli and

Eimsbüttel. When the weather's nice, the scene moves onto the streets, especially on Schulterblatt.

Restaurants

Restaurant Nil €€–€€€ On the edge of the St Pauli district, this classy retro-modern restaurant (housed in a beautiful old building which was a 1950s shoe shop) is one of the most talked about and most popular places in town, serving excellent New German cuisine. Reservations essential; book a table in the gallery if possible. Come with plenty of cash, as credit cards are not accepted. ❸ Neuer Pferdemarkt 5. ❶ 040 4397823. Ⓦ www.restaurant-nil.de ⓛ Mon, Wed, Thur 18.00–23.00, Fri & Sat 18.00–24.00, Sun 18.00–22.00. Open Tues in Dec. Bar open until 02.00 Ⓝ U-Bahn: Feldstrasse.

Bars & clubs

After Work Club at Café Schöne Aussichten Join Hamburg's trendies unwinding after work at this attractive café in the park (see opposite) to the sounds of Black Beat, House, Latin and Classics spun by top local DJs. ⓛ Thur 18.00–24.00. Admission charge.

Astra Stube Something of a cult venue, with an eclectic music line-up including punk rock, electro, reggae and pop. ❸ Max-Brauer-Allee 200/Stresemannstrasse. ❶ 43 25 06 26. Ⓝ U-Bahn: Sternschanze.

Bar Rossi A popular meeting place for Hamburg's young trendies to see and be seen. You can prop up the retro-style bar, chill out on one of the plush sofas, groove to the sounds of drum and bass on a small dance floor or simply gaze out through the large windows at the city by night. ❸ Max-Brauer-Allee 279. ⓛ Sun–Fri 18.00–03.00; Sat 18.00–04.00. ❶ 43 25 46 39. Ⓝ U-Bahn: Sternschanze.

Die Welt ist Schön 'The World is Beautiful' and so are the people who frequent this stylish modern haunt on three floors, with a terrace and dance floor. ❸ Neuer Pferdemarkt 4. ❶ 40 187 888. Ⓦ www.dieweltistschoen.net Ⓛ Sun–Wed 20.00–02.00, Thur–Sat 20.00–late. Ⓝ U-Bahn: Feldstrasse.

Summer Lounge An alternating line-up of DJs spin out the sounds in this rooftop lounge complete with open-air terrace during the summer months. ❸ Elmsbüttler Strasse 1, 2nd floor. ❶ 43 25 46 39. Ⓦ www.langnese.de/lounge. Ⓛ Thur–Sat 19.00–02.00 May–Oct. Ⓝ U-Bahn: Sternschanze.

Classical music venues

Hochschüle für Musik und Theater By the shores of the Alster, Hamburg's music academy stages regular concerts by established musicians as well as from the ranks of its own very talented students. ❸ Harveste-huder Weg 12. ❶ 42 84 80. Ⓝ U-Bahn: Hallerstrasse.

Musikhalle/Laeiszhalle

This is one of the most beautiful concert venues in Germany, with three halls offering a choice of orchestral, chamber, vocal and instrumental concerts, and sometimes jazz. ❸ Johannnes-Brahms-Platz. ❶ 34 69 20. Ⓦ www.musikhalle-hamburg.de Ⓝ U-Bahn: Gänsemarkt or Messehallen.

▶ *The Alster is a favourite spot for unwinding in the evening*

St Pauli & Altona

Where there's a port there is of course always a red-light district. Hamburg's lies just beyond the docks in the area of St Pauli. Once notorious, it is now well regulated and large parts of it have been transformed into the city's leading nightlife area with numerous theatres and respectable nightspots.

If you are only spending a couple of days in Hamburg you may not even hear the name Altona ('al-toh-nah'), let alone visit it. The 2-hour sightseeing bus trip to Blankenese (see page 126) may give you an idea of Altona as it cruises along the grand Elbchaussee riverfront road.

Altona butts up to St Pauli, though they make unlikely neighbours, from raucous red-light district to leafy executive

GUIDED WALKS

The tourist board organises a number of guided walks which cover various aspects of the St Pauli area: 'Merchants' Pride and Sailors' Dreams' departs Sunday 11.00 and Saturday 15.00 (Feb–late Nov) from Rathaus main entrance; 'Pub Crawling on the Reeperbahn' departs Fri 20.00 from Millentorplatz/St Pauli U-Bahn (Feb–Nov); 'Neon lights, Seedy Bars and Fervent Catholics – a stroll through St Pauli' departs Saturday 15.00 from the clock tower at Landungsbrücken (Feb–late Nov). 'The Beatles in St Pauli – a Magical Mystery Tour' departs Saturday 19.00 (May–late Sept) from Feldstrasse U-Bahn. Note that all tours require booking (at the tourist office) and are subject to minimum numbers and availability of English-language guides.

suburbia in just a couple of miles. Just west of the railway station Altona merges into Ottensen, and it is here that many of this area's more interesting shops, bars and restaurants are to be found.

SIGHTS & ATTRACTIONS

Dom

The huge Dom funfair sets up next to St Pauli station for around a month at a time each spring, summer and winter. It has been coming here for over a century and its roller-coasters and big wheel have become a part of the St Pauli skyline. In the wintertime (weather permitting) it also exhibits ice and snow sculptures.
ⓐ Heiligengeistfeld, St Pauli. ⓛ Mon–Thur 15.00–23.00, Fri–Sat 15.00–24.00 (summer until 00.30), Sun 14.00–23.00.
ⓦ www.hamburger-dom.de/ ⓝ U-Bahn: St Pauli.

Fischmarkt (Fish Market)

A 300-year old Hamburg institution, the Fischmarkt is as colourful a genuine street market as you will find in northern Europe and works on all levels for all people. Locals come here to pick up some astonishing bargains on exotic flowers, plants, fruits vegetables, and of course fish, from garrulous noisy stall holders; revellers come fresh off the Reeperbahn to extend their drinking and dancing; tourists come to browse for souvenirs, eat and drink at the dozens of refreshment stalls and listen to the music. The Fischmarkt hall, a striking cavernous steel and glass structure on two floors, is given over for the morning to eating, drinking and live bands who play jazz, pop and anything danceable.

● *All the fun of the fair in the Heiligengeistfeld*

📍 St Pauli Fischmarkt. 🕐 Sun. 05.00–10.00 summer; 07.00–10.00 winter. Ⓝ S-Bahn: Reeperbahn (though U-Bahn/S-Bahn to Landungsbrücken and a 10-minute walk along the front is more pleasant)

Erotic Art Museum

It's obviously not for the prudish (visitors must be 16 or older) but neither is this just a glorified porn exhibition and many of its exhibits are first-class works of art. In fact this is one of the world's biggest collections of erotic art, with around 1800 pieces spanning 500 years.
📍 Bernhard-Nocht-Strasse 69, St Pauli. 🕐 31 78 410.
Ⓦ www.eroticartmuseum.de 🕐 Sun–Thur 12.00–22.00, Fri–Sat 12.00– 24.00. Admission charge. Ⓝ U-Bahn/S-Bahn: Landungsbrücken.

Altonaer Museum

This excellent museum, one of the largest collections in northern Germany, pays special attention to the Schleswig-Holstein region, and houses Germany's largest collection of old ships' figureheads. Its wide remit also covers ethnology, fine arts, arts and crafts (with complete furnished living rooms) toys and more.
📍 Museumstrasse 23, Altona. 🕐 42 811 35 82. Ⓦ www.altonaer-museum.de 🕐 Tues–Sun 11.00–18.00. Ⓝ S-Bahn: Altona.

RETAIL THERAPY

Unless porno mags, rubber underwear and 'marital aids' from the Reeperbahn, or cheap nautically themed souvenirs (the ubiquitous ship in a bottle) from the touristy kiosks on the Landungsbrücken are on your shopping list, you won't find much to buy in this part of the city. There is the city's most famous market, however, plus one or two unusual outlets that deal in the exotic wares that pass through the port.

Harry's Hamburger Hafenbasar

More of an ethnographic museum than a conventional shop, this is a fascinating mish-mash of weird and wonderful items (including masks, musical instruments, furniture, statues, jewellery, textiles and of course erotic art and objects) collected by Hamburg seafarers from all over the world. The excellent website includes pictures of many items for sale, so you can browse before visiting or shop on-line.
🅐 Erichstrasse 56, St Pauli. ❶ 31 24 82. Ⓦ www.hafenbasar.de
🕒 Tues–Sun 12.00 –18.00. Small admission charge refundable against purchases. Ⓝ U-Bahn/S-Bahn: Landungsbrücken.

AFTER DARK – ST PAULI

Nightlife on the Reeperbahn is a heady mix of variety shows, cabarets, live music venues, DJ bars, bars with lap-dancing and pole-dancing and tacky outlets showing sex videos (live sex shows have dwindled to just one or two outlets as a result of the easy availability of internet porn). Prostitutes are not allowed to solicit on the actual Reeperbahn, though they may do so off it, especially around Herbertstrasse. This is a short street that is closed off and chicaned by brick walls (so it's impossible to enter by accident) and, like Amsterdam's famous red light area, features scantily clad girls sitting in windows. No other women, nor men under 18, are allowed into the street and should they attempt to enter, risk a soaking at the entrance (courtesy of an unobtrusive first-floor guardian) followed by immediate ejection. If you are looking for live music head for Grosse Freiheit. The famous Star Club, where many rock legends of the 1960s, including The Beatles (see page 12), cut their musical teeth has long gone, but top international bands and up-and-coming groups still play on this street.

Restaurants

Fischerhaus €€ One of the area's favourite fish restaurants. Downstairs is traditional and old-fashioned dark wood fittings; upstairs is very modern with bleached wood and harbour views (book a window seat if possible), and a slightly more expensive menu. Wherever you sit you get the freshest possible fish. ⓐ St Pauli Fischmarkt 14. ⓣ 31 40 53. ⓦ www.restaurant-fischerhaus.de ⓛ Daily 11.00– 23.00. ⓝ U-Bahn/S-Bahn: Landungsbrücke.

Warsteiner Elbspeicher €€ Very attractive place right on the waterfront, where traditional and modern mix effortlessly; light and airy décor with bare brick walls and an interesting menu with classic and new fish dishes. It also has a bistro in similar style. ⓐ Grosse Elbstrasse 39. ⓣ 38 22 42. ⓦ www.warsteiner-elbspeicher.de ⓛ Daily 12.00–24.00 (last orders 22.00). ⓝ U-Bahn/S-Bahn: Landungsbrücke.

Bars

Meanie Bar & Molotow Meanie Bar is ideal if you're a bit old for a disco and don't fancy clubbing it but you would like to drop into a trendy, welcoming, bohemian bar where the DJs really get off on a broad range of toe-tapping music all the way back to the 60s (in fact they love the 60s here!). If you are tempted to shake your bootie, pop downstairs to Molotow, where they have different theme nights and live indie and punk-rock bands play. ⓐ Spielbudenplatz 5. ⓣ 31 08 45 (Molotow 31 96 087)

W www.meaniebar.de, www.molotowclub.com ⏰ Meanie Bar: Nightly 21.00–04.00. Molotow: Fri & Sat (some Suns) 23.00–04.00. Ⓝ U-Bahn: St Pauli.

Christiansens Hamburg's top cocktail bar and something of an institution, Christiansens has two very attractive branches in the St Pauli area. ⓐ Pinnasberg 60. ☎ 317 28 63. W www.christiansens.de

Das Herz von St Pauli Just off the Reeperbahn. ⓐ Spielbudenplatz 7. ☎ 42 10 33 30. ⏰ Tues–Sun 20.00–03.00. Ⓝ U-Bahn: St Pauli; S-Bahn: Reeperbahn.

Fine Drinks & Cocktails Near the Fish Market. ⓐ Pinnasberg 60. ☎ 317 28 63. ⏰ Mon–Thur 20.00–03.00, Fri 20.00–04.00, Sat 20.00–05.30. Ⓝ S-Bahn: Reeperbahn.

SHOWS

Hamburg and particularly the Reeperbahn is famous throughout Germany for its cabaret and music-hall shows – the best known being Schmidt's Tivoli. However unless you speak very good German and can pick up topical humorous references, and German slang, most of the show will go straight over your head. Similarly, Hamburg's musicals are in German only. Its latest offering, *Dirty Dancing*, features song in English but dialogue in German. On the Reeperbahn, Pulverfass is Hamburg's most famous *Travestie* (transvestite) show. There's plenty of nudity and crudity and while it helps to know some German you can get by without (expensive cover charge).

Yakshi's Bar Gorgeous bar in Hamburg's newest designer hotel, attracting a super-trendy cosmopolitan crowd. ⓐ East Hotel, Simon-Von-Utrecht-Strasse 31. ⓣ 30 99 30. ⓦ www.east-hamburg.de ⓛ 10.00–late. ⓝ U-Bahn: St Pauli; S-Bahn: Reeperbahn.

Music bars & clubs
China Lounge Very stylish club with an Oriental theme playing a sophisticated mix of soul, funk, rare grooves, big beats/bossa nova and electronic sounds. ⓐ Nobistor 14, Reeperbahn. ⓣ 31 97 66 22. ⓦ www.china-lounge.de ⓛ Thur–Sat 22.00/23.00–0.400. ⓝ S-Bahn: Reeperbahn.

Cult Get back to that disco feeling of the 70s and 80s, with occasional sounds from the 90s too, in one of the most attractive (beautifully lit vaulted church-style) interiors on the St Pauli night scene. ② Grosse Freiheit 2. ① 29 82 21 80. ⓦ www.cult-hh.de ⓛ Fri–Sat (some Suns) 23.00–0.400. ⓝ S-Bahn: Reeperbahn.

Docks House, hip-hop, R&B, dance classics and chart toppers – if you can dance to it they will play it at this huge club, which attracts up to 1200 guests at a time. Live bands and go-go dancers too.

🔻 *Neon overload in lively Grosse Freiheit*

🅐 Spielbudenplatz 19. ☎ 31 78 83 0. 🅦 www.docks.de 🕙 Fri–Sat 22.00 onwards; for other nights, see website.

Funky Pussy Club Very popular with Hamburg students, whose art academy helped design and refurbish it recently. R&B, hip-hop and dance classics. Every Thursday is College Night, with very cheap drinks. Hip-hop, R&B, soul and house wth Latin dance tunes on Saturdays.
🅐 Grosse Freiheit 34. ☎ 31 42 36. 🅦 www.funkypussyclub.de
🕙 Thur–Sat 23.00–04.00. 🅝 S-Bahn: Reeperbahn.

Golden Pudel Club A well-established fixture on the Hamburg scene, this harbourside club attracts live-music fans of all creeds and is quick to pick up the latest trends. There's something different on every night, so look at the programme on the web or in *Pur* magazine (see page 32). 🅐 St Pauli Fischmarkt 27. ☎ 31 95 33 6. 🕙 Daily 22.00/23.00–04.00. 🅦 www.pudel.com 🅝 S-Bahn: Reeperbahn.

Grosse Freiheit 36 This is the main rock venue in town with big-name bands playing regularly. The Kaiserkeller downstairs is the setting for theme parties, usually rock-oriented but with exceptions such as reggae (Tues) and even psychedelic and garage. 🅐 Grosse Freiheit 36. ☎ 31 77 78 11. 🅦 www.grossefreiheit36.de 🕙 Daily; Mon from 20.00, other nights from 22.00. Live bands usually Fri, Sat from 23.00. 🅝 S-Bahn: Reeperbahn.

Halo This popular place made its name as the Betty Ford Klinik and some of Hamburg's top DJs make sure partygoers still get a first-class dose of musical medicine. Check the website for events.
🅐 Grosse Freiheit 6. ☎ 87 87 06 80. 🅦 www.haloclubbing.de
🕙 Fri, Sat 22.00–04.00. 🅝 S-Bahn: Reeperbahn.

AFTER DARK – ALTONA

Friedensallee is the place to see and be seen in Altona, with several attractive and trendy bars. Along the waterfront, all the way to Blankenese (see page 126), are some of the city's most acclaimed, and most expensive, gourmet restaurants. So why not take the U-Bahn or S-Bahn to Altona, have a drink or two there, then catch a taxi to a riverside restaurant.

Restaurants

Kleines Jacob €–€€ Part of one of Hamburg's finest small luxury hotels (see page 40), KJ occupies the old coach house and describes itself as 'a country pub (rustic decor and rows of old wine bottles) with a dash of Hamburg metropolitan flair'. In fact it's a very attractive wine bar-cum-restaurant with an open show kitchen providing superb yet uncomplicated dishes, together with a selection of tasty snacks, and excellent wines at all prices. Staff are very friendly and the service is impeccable. Great value.
ⓐ Elbchaussee 404. ⓣ 822 55 510. ⓦ ⓦ www.hotel-jacob.de
ⓛ Wed–Mon 18.00–23.00, Sun 12.00–14.30, 18.00–21.30.
ⓝ S-Bahn: Altona.

Landhaus Scherrer €€€ This Michelin-starred establishment is one of Hamburg's most famous and most acclaimed restaurants. For most people the main dining room is affordable for special occasions only but the attached Ö1 bistro is slightly less damaging to the wallet and the food is still wonderful. The building goes back to 1827 and is decorated with contemporary art. Oenophiles might like to note that there are 640 types of wine and 12,000 bottles here! ⓐ Elbchaussee 130. ⓣ 880 13 25. ⓦ www.landhausscherrer.de

🕐 Mon–Sat 12.00–15.30 (14.30 last orders), 18.30–late (23.00 last orders). 🚇 S-Bahn: Altona.

Tafelhaus €€€ Modern restaurant with a beautiful summer terrace on which to enjoy some of the city's finest food. The chef's Austrian, the cuisine is mostly German and Mediterranean with Oriental touches but don't be surprised to find Swiss, French and other influences too. 🏠 Neumühlen 17. ☎ 89 27 60. 🌐 www.tafelhaus-hamburg.de 🕐 Mon–Fri 12.00–16.00 (last orders 14.15), 19.00–24.00. Sat 19.00–24.00 (last orders 21.30). 🚇 S-Bahn: Königstrasse.

Bars

Eisenstein A former factory with bare stone walls and a high ceiling is the setting for this fashionable café-bar in front of the Zeisse-Kino cinema. Good pizzas served here. 🏠 Friedensallee 9. ☎ 390 46 06. 🕐 Daily 11.00–late. 🚇 S-Bahn: Altona.

Filmhauskneipe Nice wine, nice food, simple wooden tables and chairs, and lots of arty folks chatting about the film they have just seen, or are about to see, at the Zeisse-Kino (films usually in German only) next door. 🏠 Friedensallee 7. ☎ 90 80 25. 🕐 Daily 12.00–late. 🚇 S-Bahn: Altona.

▶ *The best view of Lübeck's Marienkirche is from the tower of neighbouring St Petri*

Blankenese

You will need to dedicate a half-day to visit Blankenese ('blanken-ay-zer'), which is Hamburg's prettiest village and a delight in summertime. Bus 36 travels straight down the Reeperbahn, goes through Altona (though you see very little of it from the bus), follows the Elbe and arrives in Blankenese half an hour or so later. The S-Bahn knocks 10 minutes off the journey time, but you should travel at least one way by bus to enjoy the river and parkland views

and to see the beautiful houses that line the Millionaire's Row of the Elbchaussee.

There are two 'sights' in Blankenese. The first is the village itself, an old fisherman's settlement set on a steep hill – a rarity in this part of the world – turned into a very desirable residential quarter in the 19th century by rich Hamburg merchants. It comprises some very pretty houses, including some which are thatched, and the

Blankenese, Hamburg's village on a hill

whole area is lovingly tended and landscaped with several parks.
The other sight is the view of the Elbe from the village.

Once you arrive in the relatively modern centre of Blankenese
you should head to the riverfront (Strandweg) which is over 75 m
(245 ft) below you. You have two options, either jump aboard mini-
bus 48 (the stop is just a few yards away from the S-Bahn station –
which is also where the no. 36 bus stops) – or you can walk. If you
want to use the bus service, these little 'mountain goats' (as they are
known locally) shuttle constantly between the station and river, so
you won't have long to wait for one. You'll see more if you walk
down, however, and even if you get a little lost it all adds to the
adventure. It's better to walk down than up for obvious reasons so
why not walk down and catch the bus up.

Follow Bahnhofstrasse south past the shops, past the church
and the marketplace and you will come to the town's famed
Treppenviertel (Steps or Staircase Quarter). Market days are
Tuesday, Wednesday (bio-market), Friday and Saturdays. There are
around 4800 steps in total, linking all the houses together, and the
longest of these staircases is the Strandtreppe, which has over 160
steps.

Once at the riverfront walk down towards the lighthouse (a
disappointingly prosaic structure for such a pretty place as
Blankenese) and you will find a small golden beach lapped by the
Elbe. In summer, or indeed almost any time when the sun shines,
cafés set table and chairs outside and there's quite a seaside
atmosphere.

On the bus back up get off at the Süllberg, the hill at the very top
of the town. It's not that high but as it rises so steeply you get great
views from here over the Elbe and the rest of Blankenese. A castle
has stood guard over the Elbe at this point since 1060 and the

present structure, built in the late 19th century, is now incorporated into a luxury hotel, whose terrace is open to visitors. From the Hotel Süllberg it's only a 5–10-minute walk back to the centre or there is a bus stop outside on the main road.

🚍 Bus no. 36 from Mönckebergstrasse or S-Bahn Blankenese from Hbf (line S1).

TAKING A BREAK

Hotel Süllberg The hotel, the gourmet restaurant and the views are all 5-star at this splendid castle-like hotel at the top of the hill. Take a coffee on the terrace and watch boats of every nation sailing up and down the Elbe. ❸ Süllbergsterrasse 12, Blankenese. ☎ 86 62 520. 🕐 All hours.

Kajüte SB12 Friendly little cheap-and-cheerful café on the front, by the lighthouse. In summer their tables spill onto the sands and this is a favourite meeting place for drinks and cheap eats, renowned for its *Bratkartoffelgerichte* (roast potato dishes). ❸ Strandweg 79, Blankenese. ☎ 866 42 430. 🕐 Daily Mon–Sat 10.00–late, Sun 12.00–21.00.

Witthüs It's slightly out of the centre of the village but this idyllic thatched tearoom in the beautiful Hirsch Park is well worth the detour and a perfect end to a day in Blankenese. The food is superb quality and you won't find a nicer setting anywhere in Hamburg (or perhaps anywhere ...) than their terrace. ❸ Elbchaussee 499a, Hirschpark, Mühlenberg entrance. ☎ 86 01 73. 🌐 www.witthues.de 🕐 Café: Mon–Sat 14.00–23.00, Sun and hols 10.00–23.00. Restaurant: Tues–Sun 19.00–23.00.

Lübeck

Lübeck is 59 km (37 miles) north-east of Hamburg. In the late Middle Ages it was one of Europe's richest cities and far more important than Hamburg. Its wealth came from its position as 'Queen of the Hanse', head of the Hanseatic League, the trading alliance of Dutch and North German cities which at its peak numbered over 160 members and controlled the highly lucrative Baltic Sea routes. When the monopoly of the Hanseatic League was broken and other routes became more important Lübeck's star waned. However, it has retained its maritime standing; today it is still the busiest German port on the Baltic Sea and a significant industrial centre (though visitors to the Old Town will see neither of these facets).

Lübeck's historic heart, the Old Town, is a small and compact island girdled by canals. Day-visitors can cover its highlights on foot quite comfortably. However, if you have more than a single day there is more to see and do, including several museums and boat trips. If you are staying overnight there are plenty of good bars, restaurants and an active nightlife scene.

Ⓝ Trains run every half hour or so from Hamburg Hbf and take around 50 mins. From Lübeck Hbf it is a 5-minute walk to the centre of the Old Town.

SIGHTS & ATTRACTIONS

Holstentor (Holstein Gate)

This fairy-tale twin-turreted gateway was built in 1478 when Lübeck was at its peak. It is the symbol of the city and the sheer bulk of this fortification, which once held 48 cannons, gives an idea as to Lübeck's historic importance. Today it is home to a small museum,

Museum für Natar
und Umwelt

Dom

Völkerkunde-
Sammlung

Wallstr.

Mühlenbrücke

An der Mauer

Dankwartsgrube

Mühlenstr.

Krähenstr.

Balauerföhr

Wahmstr.

Marlesgrube

An der Obertrave

Petrikirche

Museum für
Figurentheater

Holstentor

Wallstr.

Possehlstr.

Holstentor-
platz

Lindenplatz

Sandstr.

Huxstr.

Markt

Holstenstr.

Fischstraße

Dr.-Julius-leber-str.

Rathaus

Schüsselbuden

Schabbelhaus

An der Untertrave

Boat Tours

Fleischhauerstr.

Königstr.

Behnhaus/
Drägerhaus

Günter-
Grass-Haus

Buddenbrookhaus

Marienkirche

Mengstr.

Willy-Brandt-Allee

Heiligen-Geist-
Hospital

St Jakobi

Schiffergesellschaft

Breite Str.

Engelswisch

Fischergrube

An der Untertrave

Martinstr.

Kanalstr.

Wakenitzmauer

Langer Lohberg

Grosse Burgstrasse

Gustav
Radbruch
Platz

Burgtorbr.

Hubbrücke

> **LÜBECK REBUILT**
> Although Lübeck is frequently described as a beautiful, historic and unspoiled city, a quarter of it was lost to Allied bombing in 1942 and much of its old centre had to be rebuilt. Today it is on the UNESCO list as a World Heritage Site. However, not all the town was rebuilt in the old style and the main Holstenstrasse in particular is a typically ugly 1960s-style thoroughfare, complete with fast food outlets and cheap shops.

which gives a brief introduction to the town. Immediately behind the gate is a row of elegant 16th-century gabled houses which were once Salzspeicher (salt warehouses). One of these has been converted into a shop, the rest are closed to the public.

ⓐ Holstentorplatz ⓣ (0451) 1224 129. ⓦ www.museen.luebeck.de ⓛ Tues–Fri 10.00–16.00, Sat –Sun 11.00–17.00 Jan–Mar and Oct–Dec; Tues–Fri 11.00–17.00, Sat–Sun 10.00–17.00 Apr–Sept. Admission charge.

Petrikirche (St Peter's Church)

Now deconsecrated, this 13th-century church is used for art exhibitions, and is worth noting for its 50 m (152 ft) tower, which is open to visitors as a viewing point. The panorama from here is not great but you do get an idea of the town's layout.

ⓐ Schmiederstrasse. ⓣ (0451) 397 730. ⓛ Tues–Sun 11.00–16.00 (during exhibitions until 17.00). Admission charge to tower.

Rathaus (Town Hall)

This splendid, sprawling late medieval complex was begun in the

13th century and features arcades and spires and the town's hallmark bands of glazed and unglazed brickwork. It is the oldest working town hall in Germany. The two unusual huge 'portholes' in the brick screen above the town hall were designed to let the fierce Baltic sea wind howl through instead of blowing the wall down. On the main street running along the side of the building don't miss the ornate Renaissance staircase of 1594. Opposite here is another of the town's most famous institutions, the Niederegger shop, museum and café (see pages 140 and 141).

ⓐ Rathausplatz. ❶ (0451) 122 10 05. ◗ Guided tours Mon–Fri 11.00, 12.00, 15.00 (German only). Charge for tours.

An der Untertrave & Mengstrasse

Here along the waterfront you will find several historic traditional sailing ships moored in front of beautiful gabled houses, many dating from the 17th century, including the Tesdorpf-Haus (on the corner with Mengstrasse), which is the town's oldest wine importer. Turn into Mengstrasse, a fine street full of historic houses, and take a look in at no. 48–50, the Schabbelhaus (see After Dark, page 141).

Marienkirche (St Mary's Church)

This imposing edifice, constructed 1250–1350 and topped by twin spires soaring 125 m (410 ft) high, is one of the finest Gothic churches in the country and the third largest in all Germany. There are several highlights within, including its vaulted ceiling, the world's largest mechanical organ and its astronomical clock. The great bells, brought crashing down in 1942, remain where they fell, making a lasting impression on today's visitors as well as on the church floor, where they lie in pieces.

ⓐ Schüsselbuden 13. ❶ (0451) 397 700. ◗ Daily 10.00–16.00.

Heiligen-Geist-Hospital (Hospice of the Holy Spirit)

One of the oldest social institutions in Germany, and until very recently one of the oldest hospitals in Europe, this splendid complex is a church with a hospice attached, built by the city's wealthy merchants in 1280. Its 14th-century church wall paintings are some of the brightest and most important medieval examples in northern Germany. Behind the church is a huge hall containing little wooden *Kabäuschen* (cabins), where until the 1970s old and infirm people were cared for. It is also worth looking below, in the former wine cellars, now occupied by a restaurant (see page 142).

ⓐ Am Koberg. ☎ (0451) 122 20 40. ⏰ Tues–Sun. 10.00–17.00 Apr–Sept; 10.00–16.00 Oct–Mar.

MUSEUMS-CARD

A Lübeck Museums-Card costs €4 and entitles you to or discounted (usually half-price) admission at most museums, which means that after two to three visits the card pays for itself.

Hidden courtyards

A short distance from the Heiligen-Geist-Hospital, in Glockengiesserstrasse, are two more examples of the city's long history of charitable institutions in the form of 17th-century almshouses. The Füchtings-Hof at no. 23 was built for the widows of sea captains, the Glandorp-Hof, entrance next to no. 49, for the widows of craftsmen. Each is set in an idyllic courtyard – you may enter but do heed the signs and do not go any further than you are invited.

▲ *The Marienkirche looms behind the facade of the Rathaus*

St Jakobi/Jakobikirche (St James' Church)

'The Seafarer's Church' escaped the bombing of 1942 and is famous for its art treasures, most notably the 15th-century Brömse Altar and its beautifully preserved 14th-century wall paintings. It is also renowned for its organ music and features two 16th-century organs. In the north tower chapel the damaged lifeboat of the Pamir, which sank in 1957 with the loss of 80 (mostly young) lives, is a touching memorial to those lost at sea.

🅐 Breitstrasse/Jacobikirchhof 5. 🕐 (0451) 30 80 10. Ⓦ www.stjakobi-luebeck.de 🕒 Daily. 10.00–16.00 Apr–Sept; 10.00–15.00 Oct–Mar.

Dom (Cathedral)

Lübeck's Cathedral is overlooked by most day-visitors as it is at the 'wrong' (southern) end of the Old Town, away from the other attractions. It was built in 1230 but badly damaged in 1942 and restoration has swept away its ancient atmosphere. In the churchyard are two museums: the Museum für Natur und Umwelt (Museum of Nature and the Environment) and the Völkerkundesammlung (Folklore collection).

Dom ⓐ Domkirchhof. ⓦ www.domzuluebeck.de
🕑 Daily 10.00–18.00 Apr–Oct; 10.00–16.00 Oct–Mar.
Museum für Natur und Umwelt ⓐ Mühlendamm 1–3.
ⓘ (0451) 122 41 22. ⓦ www.museenluebeck.de 🕑 Tues–Fri
09.00–17.00, Sun 10.00–17.00 Apr–Sept; Tues–Fri 09.00–16.00, Sat-
Sun 10.00–16.00 Oct–Mar. Admission charge.
Völkerkundesammlung ⓐ Zeughaus am Dom, Parade 10.
ⓘ (0451) 122 43 42. ⓦ www.museenluebeck.de Tues–Sun
10.00–17.00. Admission charge.

Museum für Figurentheater (Puppet Theatre Museum)

Set in a terrace of five historic half-timbered houses this fascinating,
colourful and often exotic collection claims to be the world's largest
puppet theatre museum. It features around 5000 puppets and
props (including posters, stages and barrel organs) from all over the
world and has its own puppet theatre next door, though
performances are only in German.
ⓐ Kolk 16. ⓘ (0451) 786 26 and 700 60. ⓦ www.fritzfey.de
🕑 Daily 10.00–18.00. Admission charge.

Boat trips

Boat trips around Lübeck Harbour give you an excellent waterside
view of the many fine houses that line the canals. In summer you
might like to take an excursion to the Baltic Sea resort of
Travemünde, 20 km (13 miles) north-east of Lübeck. There is a
charming old town here, with many half-timbered houses and a
long sandy beach. All trips depart from An der Untertraven.

▶ *The world of theatre in miniature at the Museum für Figurentheater*

CULTURE

Lübeck has a strong artistic and literary background, and is the home town of Thomas Mann and Günter Grass, both winners of the Nobel Prize for Literature (1929 and 1999 respectively).

Buddenbrookhaus

Built in 1758, this beautiful house was the home of Johann Siegmund Mann, grandfather of the city's two famous sons, the author Thomas Mann (1875–1955) – best known for *Death in Venice* (1912) – and his less celebrated literary brother, Heinrich Mann (1871–1950). It is now a centre dedicated to their works.

ⓐ Mengstrasse 4. ☎ (0451) 122 41 92 ⓦ buddenbrookehaus.de
🕐 Daily. 10.00–18.00 Apr–Oct; 10.00–17.00 Nov–Mar. Admission charge.

Günter-Grass-Haus

Not just a study of Grass as an author but also his works an artist and sculptor.

ⓐ Glockengiesserstrasse 21. ⓦ www.Guenter-Grass-Haus.de 🕐 Daily. 10.00–18.00 Apr–Dec; 11.00–17.00 Jan–Mar. Admission charge.

Museum Behnhaus/Drägerhaus

The Behnhaus is a museum and gallery of 19th- and 20th-century paintings, crafts and sculptures; the adjacent Drägerhaus (same entrance) is a perfectly preserved 18th-century house with Biedermeier arts and crafts pieces.

ⓐ Königstrasse 9–11. ☎ (0451) 122 4148. 🕐 Tues–Sun 10.00–17.00

🔊 *Although extensively reconstructed, Lübeck has an old-world feel*

Apr–Sept; Tues–Fri 10.00–16.00, Sat–Sun 11.00–17.00 Oct–Mar.
Admission charge.

RETAIL THERAPY

Most of Lübeck's shops are on Breit Strasse and Königstrasse and are
small and specialist, though there is a branch of Karstadt
department store in the centre. There are several good food and
drink outlets, typical Lübeck souvenirs being Lübecker Rotspon wine,
Lübecker nut cake and marzipan.

Christmas in Lübeck

Lübeck is famous for its Christmas Market, centring on the town hall
square. The highlight of the town at this period, however, is the
Heiligen-Geist-Hospital, which hosts a very popular Christmas
Crafts Market, attracting crafts vendors from all over northern
Germany. Many of these set up their stalls in the tiny cabins of the
former hospice (see page 134). Expect to queue.

Niederegger

Choose from over 100 types of pastries and cakes and 300 kinds of
marzipan confectionery (Lübeck has been the home of marzipan for
over 500 years) at the world's most famous marzipan shop.
ⓐ Breite Strasse 89 ① (0451) 53 01 126. Ⓦ www.niederegger.de
① Mon–Fri 09.00–19.00, Sat 09.00–18.00, Sun 10.00–18.00.

TAKING A BREAK

There are good restaurants, bars and cafés all over the town centre.
Mühlenstrasse has the greatest concentration.

Café Niederegger This old–fashioned Grand Salon-style café is perfect for sweet indulgence. ⓐ Breite Strasse 89. ⓣ (0451) 53 01 126. ⓦ www.niederegger.de ⓛ Mon–Fri 09.00–19.00, Sat 09.00–18.00, Sun 10.00–18.00.

Im alten Zolln The fabric of the city's oldest pub goes back to at least 1589 and there's usually a cosy atmosphere, with locals and tourists rubbing shoulders. Inexpensive snacks at lunchtime and live music on several nights make this a good place to visit at any time. ⓐ Mühlenstrasse 93–95. ⓣ (0451) 7 2395. ⓦ www.zolln.de ⓛ Daily 12.00–late.

KartoffelKeller If the weather is good you don't have to go below ground to enjoy the KartoffelKeller (Potato Cellar), as they have a charming terrace too. There are plenty of inventive potato dishes alongside old-fashioned bistro favourites. ⓐ Koberg 8. ⓣ (0451) 76234. ⓦ www.kartoffel-keller.de ⓛ Daily 12.00–24.00.

Ratskeller Descend to the vaults beneath the Rathaus (town hall) for hearty local specialities and typical North German dishes. ⓐ Markt 13 ⓣ (0451) 720 44. ⓛ daily 12.00–24.00.

AFTER DARK

Lübeck is a busy cultural centre with nightlife from church concerts to Irish pubs and punk bands. There are two free monthly listings magazines; *Heute Events & Kultur* (in English and German) and *Ultimo* (German only). The latter is also available online: ⓦ www.ultimo-luebeck.de

Haus der Schiffergesellschaft (House of the Sea Captains' Guild) €€
Entering this dark, atmospherically lit beamed space feels as if you have descended below deck on a 16th-century galleon. Founded in 1535 as a meeting room, it is festooned with maritime antiques and large time-worn model ships hang from the ceiling. It is nearly always busy and it's best to get a table well away from the doors as curious visitors are constantly looking in. Despite being a tourist attraction in its own right the food is good quality and the menu specialises in fish. ⓐ Breit Strasse 2. ⓣ (0451) 76 776.
ⓦ www.schiffergesellschaft.de. ⓛ Tues–Sun 10.00–24.00.

Historischer Weinkeller €€€ The atmospheric 12th-century former wine cellar of the Holy Ghost Hospice is now home to a wine bar, a gourmet restaurant and the cheaper KartoffelKeller (see page 141). The restaurant serves top class international and German dishes at reasonable prices. ⓐ Koberg 8. ⓣ (0451) 76234 ⓦ www.historischer-weinkeller-hl.de ⓛ Daily 12.00–24.00.

Schabbelhaus €€€ Imagine you are an upper-class Hanseatic merchant in the grand antique-filled interior of this beautifully preserved 16th/17th-century house. Excellent regional cuisine and the lunchtime fixed-price menu is a bargain. ⓐ Mengstrasse 48–52. ⓣ (0451) 720 11. ⓦ www.schabbelhaus.de ⓛ Mon–Sat 12.00–14.30, 18.00–23.00.

ⓞ *After eight centuries, Hamburg continues to welcome ships of all nations*

PRACTICAL
information

Directory

GETTING THERE

By air

You can fly direct to Hamburg from all London airports and most major provincial airports in the UK. Flight time is around 2 hours. The cheapest flights are often provided by German Wings (from Gatwick) and Easyjet (from Bristol). British Airways and KLM provide scheduled flights. Ryanair flies to Lübeck from Stansted.

Package breaks may be worth considering if you want 4- or 5-star luxury, as accommodation in Hamburg's top hotels can be expensive. If you are happy with booking your own two- or three-star hotel and you can get a cheap flight, however, a package is unlikely to offer you a saving. The tourist board offer a number of *Happy Hamburg* packages, click on Ⓦ www.hamburg-tourism.de for details.

British Airways Ⓦ www.ba.com

Easyjet Ⓦ www.easyjet.co.uk

German Wings Ⓦ www.germanwings.com

KLM Ⓦ www.klm.com

Ryanair Ⓦ www.ryanair.co.uk

By rail

There is no direct rail link between the UK and Hamburg. Journeys involve a Eurostar trip from London Waterloo International to Paris or Brussels. If you do not want to travel overnight you will have to change at Brussels and Cologne; if you do take an overnight train then you can change at either Paris or Brussels. The standard rail fare is much more expensive than the no-frills airfare.

Eurostar Reservations (UK) ☏ 08705 186186 Ⓦ www.eurostar.com

Thomas Cook European Rail Timetable ℹ (UK) 01733 416477; (USA) 1 800 322 3834. Ⓦ www.thomascookpublishing.com

Driving

DFDS Seaways operates a car ferry from Harwich to Cuxhaven, approx (125 km) 75 miles from Hamburg. The boat departs Harwich at 16.00 and arrives in Cuxhaven at 11.30 the next day.

DFDS Seaways Ⓦ www.dfdsseaways.co.uk

ENTRY FORMALITIES
Documentation

Visas are not required by citizens of the USA, Canada, Republic of Ireland, Australia, New Zealand, the UK and members of other EU countries for visits of less than 3 months. South African nationals do require a visa. Citizens of the UK and of all countries except other EU states require a valid passport. EU citizens travelling without a passport need only a national identity card. It is recommended that you always carry a passport anyway.

Customs

There are no customs controls at borders for visitors from EU countries. Visitors from EU countries can bring in, or take out, goods without any restrictions on quantity or value, as long as these goods are for personal use only. Visitors from outside the EU are subject to the following restrictions. Most personal effects and the following items are duty-free: a portable typewriter; one video camera or two still cameras with ten rolls of film each; a portable radio, a tape recorder, and a laptop computer, provided they show signs of use; 400 cigarettes or 50 cigars or 250 g (9 oz) of tobacco; 2 litres (0.52

gallons) of wine or 1 litre (0.26 gallons) of liquor per person over 17 years old; fishing gear; one bicycle; skis; tennis or squash racquets; and golf clubs.

As entry requirements and customs regulations are subject to change, you should always check the current situation with your local travel agent, airline or a German embassy or consulate before you leave. For current information on visas and customs requirements contact: German Department of Foreign Affairs (Auswärtiges Amt): Ⓦ www.auswaertiges-amt.de.

MONEY

The euro (€) is the official currency in Germany. €1 = 100 cents. It comes in notes of €5, €10, €20, €50, €100, €200 and €500. Coins are in denominations of €1 and €2, and 1, 2, 5, 10, 20 and 50 cents.

ATM (Geldautomat) machines are readily found at airports, railway stations, shopping centres and in downtown areas. They are the quickest and most convenient way to obtain cash. Instructions on use are available in English and other major European languages. As well as in downtown areas, there are banks or bureaux de change at airports and main railway stations in the cities.

The most widely accepted credit cards are Eurocard and Mastercard, though other major credit cards such as Visa and American Express are also commonly accepted. But note that many smaller businesses, including some restaurants, bars and small hotels may not accept credit card payment. This is especially the case outside Hamburg, in smaller towns. As a rule, supermarkets do not accept credit cards. It is advisable to always carry some cash along with your credit card. Traveller's cheques are best cashed at a Wechselbüro (exchange bureau), because many banks won't change them.

HEALTH, SAFETY & CRIME

The standard of food and drink hygiene is as high – if not higher – than anywhere in northern Europe and visitors should have no problems. Likewise, the quality of healthcare and paramedical aid befits one of Europe's wealthiest cities. You must of course make sure you are insured against illness and accident before travelling, to avoid hefty bills.

Thanks to a reciprocal healthcare agreement, nationals of EU countries and some other countries can get reduced-price, sometimes free, medical treatment in Germany on presentation of a valid European Health Insurance Card (EHIC), the replacement for the previous E111 form. This card gives access to state-provided medical treatment only. Apply online (🔵 www.dh.gov.uk/travellers) for an EHIC and allow at least 2–3 weeks until you receive the card. On top of this, private medical insurance is still advised and is essential for non-EU visitors. Dental treatment is not available free of charge.

Crimes against tourists in Hamburg are rare and problems are usually confined to the backstreets of the red-light district (see page 117). All streets in the city centre are safe by day and the vast majority are safe by night, though visitors should be aware that the St Georg district is known for prostitution and drug dealing and that the Kircheallee exit of the Hauptbahnhof is frequented by lowlife after dark. Take the usual big city precautions and you should have no problems. Police are usually present on the main streets, wear a dark navy uniform and for the most part are approachable and helpful to visitors.

OPENING HOURS

Most museums and galleries are closed on Monday and open from

Tuesday to Sunday 10.00–17.00 or 18.00. Traditional shop opening hours are Monday to Saturday 09.00/10.00–17.30/18.00. Some shops close at 14.00 on Saturday. On Mönckebergstrasse and in the malls, however, most shops open longer hours, usually Monday to Saturday 10.00–20.00.

Office hours are Monday to Friday 08.30/09.00–17.00/18.00. Restaurants open from around 12.00 to 15.00 for lunch and 19.00–23.00 for dinner. Some bars open from around 12.00 and stay open through the day, others open for the evening only at around 18.00/19.00. Several do not have set closing hours though 04.00 is the latest that most are permitted to open. In the St Pauli district most bars are open until 04.00, some even later.

TOILETS

Public toilets are not that common, however where you do find them they are generally well kept (you may have to pay a small amount which goes to their upkeep). It is probably best to avoid any you may find in the red-light district. Any bar, restaurant department store or shopping mall will have a toilet for clients.

CHILDREN

Hamburg is not an obvious place for children but, the red-light district aside, there are no reasons why you shouldn't bring them here for a city break. Good places to go are:

- **Hagenbecks Zoo** One of the best, and with a small kiddies' area (see page 105).

- **Planten un Blomen park** (page 102) has several children's amusement areas.

- Teens will enjoy the frisson of fear and gore at the **Hamburg Dungeon** (see page 97).

- If you want a family-friendly after-dark activity go to the **Dom** funfair (see page 114) when it is in town, or the **Planetarium Hamburg** (see page 107).

🔺 *Treat the kids to a night at the Dom*

- Trainspotters of all ages will love **Miniatur Wunderland** (see page 97), while older children and enquiring minds might like the **Hamburg History Museum** (see page 69) – which also has a huge model railway, though it only operates at certain times.

- Some children will love a **boat trip** around the harbour (see pages 90–92) or around the Alster (see page 64), and exploring the **U-434 Russian submarine** (see page 94) might be a good option.

- In the summer you can go to the riverside beaches at Övelgönne or Blankenese (see page 126) or take a trip to the large beach at the seaside resort of Travemünde, not far from Lubeck.

- Winter is magical for the Christmas Markets, particularly if it snows (see page 11).

There are very few restaurants that make special provisions for children. However, well-behaved offspring will always be welcome and most places will scale down portion sizes if you request it. If you are concerned whether they will enjoy German food – any child who likes hot dogs will enjoy the ubiquitous *Würstchen* (frankfurter-style sausages).

COMMUNICATIONS
Phones
Coin-operated public phones are rare; far more common are card-operated phones. Telephone cards (*Telefonkarten*) can be bought at any post office and some shops such as bookshops or kiosks at railway stations. A display shows how much credit is left.

Instructions on how to use public telephones are written in English in phone booths for international calls. Otherwise, lift up the receiver, insert the telephone card and dial the number.

When making an international call, dial the international code you require and drop the initial zero of the area code you are ringing. The international dialling code for calls from Germany to Australia is 0061, to the UK 0044, to the Irish Republic 00353, to South Africa 0027, to New Zealand 0064, and to the USA and Canada 001.

The code for dialling to Germany from abroad, after the access code (00 in most countries) is 49. To call Hamburg from abroad, the code is 49 40.

To call Frankfurt from within Germany dial 040 and then the number, unless calling from Hamburg itself, when there is no need to dial 040. In this book, numbers in the Hamburg area are given without the area code; Hamburg telephone numbers range from 6 to 8 digits. All numbers outside Hamburg have been quoted with the area code in brackets, e.g. (0451) for a Lübeck number.

Post

Postal services are quick and efficient. Stamps can be purchased from most places that sell postcards and from post offices. The main post office is opposite the Hauptbahnhof, Kirchenallee exit. Post boxes are yellow. It costs €1 to send a postcard from Germany to the UK.

Internet

Internet access points are spreading with several internet cafés around the centre of town and may of the trendier bars and cafés offering wi-fi areas where you can surf free of wires with your own notebook PC.

ELECTRICITY

The supply nationally is 220 volts (AC), 50 Hertz. Round-ended, two-pronged adapters are needed for UK and North American appliances; the latter will also need a transformer for the voltage difference.

TRAVELLERS WITH DISABILITIES

The Hamburg tourist office website is an excellent source of information. Click on Ⓦ www.hamburg-tourism.de, go to Hamburg Info (on the top red bar) then HH Handicapped Persons. There you will find comprehensive advice on transport, accommodation, eating out, events, shows and how to enjoy Hamburg with minimum hassle. For information in your own country, contact:

Holiday Care UK-based advice. ❶ 0845 124 9971
Ⓦ www.holidaycare.org.uk
Tripscope Another useful source for UK travellers. ❸ Alexandra House, Albany Road, Brentford, Middlesex TW8 0NE.
❶ 0845 758 5641. Ⓦ www.tripscope.org.uk
Irish Wheelchair Association ❸ Blackheath Drive, Clontarf, Dublin 3.
❶ 01 818 6400. Ⓦ www.iwa.ie
Society for the Advancement of Travelers with Handicaps (SATH)
North American-based travellers. ❸ 347 5th Avenue, New York, NY 10016, USA. ❶ 212 447 7284. Ⓦ www.sath.org
Access-able Ⓦ www.access-able.com
Australian Council for Rehabilitation of the Disabled (ACROD)
❸ PO Box 60, Curtin, ACT 2605; Suite 103, 1st Floor, 1–5 Commercial Road, Kings Grove, 2208. ❶ 02 6282 4333. Ⓦ www.acrod.org.au
Disabled Persons Assembly For New Zealand-based travellers.
❸ 4/173–175 Victoria Street, Wellington, New Zealand.
❶ 04 801 9100. Ⓦ www.dpa.org.nz

FURTHER INFORMATION

Hamburg tourist office

Main office 🚇 Hauptbahnhof (main railway station), in at the back of the station, Kirchenallee entrance. 🕐 Mon–Sat 08.00–21.00, Sun and hols 10.00–18.00.

There is a dedicated visitor telephone number (📞 300 51 300, open daily 08.00–20.00) which deals with hotel reservations, tickets for events, package tours as well as general enquiries. See also the excellent 🌐 www.hamburg-tourism.de

There are four other offices in Hamburg:

St Pauli Landungsbrücken 🚇 Landungsbrücken, between piers 4 and 5. 🕐 Daily.10.00–18.00 Nov–Mar; 08.00–18.00 Apr–Oct. Open all year Tues, Thur, Fri & Sat until 19.00.

Airport 🚇 Terminal 1 and 2, Arrivals area. 🕐 Daily 05.30–23.00.

CCH Ticket Office Dammtor Station 🚇 Dag-Hammerskjöld-Platz. 🕐 Mon–Fri 08.00–19.45, Sat 10.00–16.00.

Alster Lounge, Jungfernstieg Station. 🚇 Jungfernstieg. 🕐 Sun–Fri 09.00–18.30 Apr–Oct; 10.00–18.00 Nov–Mar. Sat 10.00–16.00 all year.

To find out what's on, pick up a free copy of the monthly English-language *Hamburg Guide* available from several hotels and shopping mall, or go online 🌐 www.hamburg-guide.de

Lübeck

Lübeck Tourist Office 🚇 Holstentorplatz 1. 🌐 www.luebeck-tourismus.de. 🕐 Mon–Fri. 09.30- 18.00, Sat 10.00–15.00, public holidays 10.00–14.00 Jan–May, Oct, Nov; Mon–Fri. 09.30–19.00, Sat 10.00–15.00 Jun–Sept & Dec. Sun. and public holidays 10.00–14.00.

Useful phrases

Although English is widely spoken in Hamburg, these words and phrases may come in handy. See also the phrases for specific situations in other parts of the book.

English	German	*Approx. pronunciation*
BASICS		
Yes	Ja	*Yah*
No	Nein	*Nine*
Please	Bitte	*Bitter*
Thank you	Danke	*Danke*
Hello	Hallo	*Hallo*
Goodbye	Auf Wiedersehen	*Owf Veederzeyhen*
Excuse me	Entschuldigen Sie	*Entshooldigen zee*
Sorry	Entschuldigung	*Entshooldigoong*
That's okay	Das stimmt	*Das shtimt*
To	Nach	*Nakh*
From	Von	*Fon*
I don't speak German	Ich spreche kein Deutsch	*Ikh shprekher kine doitsh*
Do you speak English	Sprechen Sie Englisch?	*Shprekhen zee eng-lish?*
Good morning	Guten Morgen	*Gooten morgen*
Good afternoon	Guten Tag	*Gooten targ*
Good evening	Guten Abend	*Gooten arbent*
Goodnight	Gute Nacht	*Gooter nakht*
My name is ...	Mein Name ist ...	*Mine naamer ist ...*
DAYS & TIMES		
Monday	Montag	*Mohntagh*
Tuesday	Dienstag	*Deenstagh*
Wednesday	Mittwoch	*Mitvokh*
Thursday	Donnerstag	*Donnerstagh*
Friday	Freitag	*Frytagh*
Saturday	Samstag	*Samstagh*
Sunday	Sonntag	*Sontagh*
Morning	Morgen	*Morgen*
Afternoon	Nachmittag	*Naakhmittag*
Evening	Abend	*Aabend*
Night	Nacht	*Naakht*
Yesterday	Gestern	*Gess-tern*

English	German	Approx. pronunciation
Today	Heute	*Hoyter*
Tomorrow	Morgen	*Morgen*
What time is it?	Wie spät ist es?	*Vee shpeyt is es?*
It is ...	Es ist ...	*Es ist ...*
09.00	Neun Uhr	*Noyn oor*
Midday	Mittag	*Mittagh*
Midnight	Mitternacht	*Mitternakht*

NUMBERS

One	Eins	*Ines*
Two	Zwei	*Tsvy*
Three	Drei	*Dry*
Four	Vier	*Feer*
Five	Fünf	*Foonf*
Six	Sechs	*Zex*
Seven	Sieben	*Zeeben*
Eight	Acht	*Akht*
Nine	Neun	*Noyn*
Ten	Zehn	*Tseyn*
Eleven	Elf	*Elf*
Twelve	Zwölf	*Tsverlf*
Twenty	Zwanzig	*Tvantsikh*
Fifty	Fünfzig	*Foonftsikh*
One hundred	Hundert	*Hoondert*

MONEY

I would like to change these traveller's cheques/this currency	Ich möchte gerne diese Reisechecks/dieses Geld/wechseln	*Ikh merkhter gairner deezer ryzersheks/deezes gelt/vexseln*
Where is the nearest ATM?	Wo ist der nächste Geldautomat?	*Voh ist dair nexter geld-owtomaat?*
Do you accept credit cards?	Nehmen sie Kreditkarten an?	*Neymen zee credeetcarten an?*

SIGNS & NOTICES

Airport	Flughafen	*Floogharfen*
Rail station/Platform	Bahnhof/Bahnsteig	*Baanhof/Baanshtykh*
Smoking/non-smoking	Raucher/Nichtraucher	*Raukher/nikhtraukher*
Toilets	Toiletten	*Toletten*
Ladies/Gentlemen	Damen/Herren	*Daamen/Herren*
Subway	Die U-Bahn	*Dee Oo-baan*

Emergencies

EMERGENCY NUMBERS
Feuerwehr (Fire service) ☎ 112
Notarzt (Emergency doctor, ambulance) ☎ 112
Polizei (Police) ☎ 110
First Aid 24-hour service ☎ 24 82 81

HEALTH
If you need a doctor or dentist, you can check the local phone book under *Ärtzte* (doctors) or *Zahnärzte* (dentists). Otherwise, if you want to find an English-speaking doctor (most doctors will speak at least some English), ask at the local tourist office or contact your nearest embassy or consulate. The latter usually have lists of English-speaking doctors and dentists, and can also offer assistance in case of emergencies.

Hospitals (Krankenhäuser) with emergency departments
Krankenhaus Bethesda ⓐ Glindersweg. ☎ 46 680.
University Hospital (also for emergency dental treatment)
ⓐ Eppendorf. ☎ 42 80 30.

Pharmacies (*Apotheken*)
Pharmacies are easily spotted by their green cross signs. German pharmacists and are qualified to offer medical advice on minor health problems which would be the business of a doctor in Britain. Information on the after-hour emergency and weekend pharmacy service (*Apothekennotdienst*) is displayed in front of every pharmacy. Addresses are also listed in local papers and on the internet at ⓦ www.frankfurt.de.

LOST PROPERTY

Lost Property Office ⓐ Bäckerbreitergang 73. ⓣ 35 18 51.

CONSULATES & EMBASSIES

Australian Embassy ⓐ Wallstrasse 76–79, Berlin. ⓣ (030) 88 00 880.
ⓦ www.australian-embassy.de

British Consulate ⓐ Harvestehuder Weg 8a. ⓣ 44 80 320.
ⓦ www.britischebotschaft.de/en/consular/hamburg/

Canadian Consulate ⓐ 5th Floor, Ballindamm 35 ⓣ 46 00 270.
ⓦ www.dfait-maeci.gc.ca

Irish Consulate ⓐ Feldbrunnenstrasse 43. ⓣ 44 18 62 13.

New Zealand Consulate ⓐ Heimhuderstrasse 56 ⓣ 442 55 50.

South African Embassy ⓐ Tiergartenstrasse 18, Berlin.
ⓣ (030) 22 07 30. ⓦ www.suedafrika.org/en/kontakt.php

US Consulate ⓐ Alsterufer 27/28 ⓣ 411 71 100.
ⓦ http://hamburg.usconsulate.gov

EMERGENCY PHRASES

Help! Hilfe! *Heelfe!*   **Fire!** Feuer! *Foyer!*   **Stop!** Halt! *Halt!*

Call an ambulance/a doctor/the police/the fire service!
Rufen Sie bitte einen Krankenwagen/einen Arzt/
die Polizei/die Feuerwehr!
*Roofen zee bitter inen krankenvaagen/inen artst/
dee politsye/dee foyervair!*

INDEX

Paul Murphy would like to thank Elif Lavas and the staff of the Hamburg Tourismus for the generous assistance that they provided with the research of this guidebook. Thanks too to the following hotels: Hotel Side, Hotel Kempinski Grand Atlantic; Hotel Elysee; Hotel Louis C Jacob; Hotel Hafen Hamburg.

The publishers would like to thank the following individuals and organisations for supplying their copyright photographs for this book. A1 Pix: pages 1, 5, 7, 17, 21, 33, 42, 47, 73, 79, 83, 103, 106, 111, 120 and 143. Björn Busch: page 12. Paul Murphy: pages 10, 15, 18, 25, 30, 35, 45, 49, 57, 61, 65, 71, 93, 100, 115, 125, 126, 135, 137, 139 and 149.

Proofreader: Angela Chevalier-Watts

Copy-editor: Stephen York

Send your thoughts to
books@thomascook.com

- **Found a great bar, club, shop or must-see sight that we don't feature?**

- **Like to tip us off about any information that needs a little updating?**

- **Want to tell us what you love about this handy little guidebook and more importantly how we can make it even handier?**

Then here's your chance to tell all! Send us ideas, discoveries and recommendations today and then look out for your valuable input in the next edition of this title. As an extra 'thank you' from Thomas Cook Publishing, you'll be automatically entered into our exciting monthly prize draw.

Email the above address (stating the book's title) or write to: CitySpots Project Editor, Thomas Cook Publishing, PO Box 227, Unit 15/16, Coningsby Road, Peterborough PE3 8SB, UK.